Soups & Salads

igloobooks

Published in 2016
by Igloo Books Ltd
Cottage Farm
Sywell
NN6 0BJ
www.igloobooks.com

Food photography and recipe development:
© Stockfood, The Food Media Agency
Cover image © Scott Simms / Getty Images

HUN001 0216
2 4 6 8 10 9 7 5 3 1
ISBN: 978-1-78557-543-3

Cover designed by Nicholas Gage
Interiors designed by Charles Wood-Penn
Edited by Natalie Baker

Printed and manufactured in China

Contents

Soups

Vegetable
Soups

Tomato and Basil Soup

SERVES 4

PREPARATION TIME 10 MINUTES

COOKING TIME 30–35 MINUTES

INGREDIENTS

2 tbsp olive oil
1 medium onion, finely chopped
1 stick of celery, finely chopped
salt and freshly ground black pepper
1 kg / 2 lb 4 oz / 4 cups ripe vine tomatoes,
    washed, cored and quartered
1 ½ tsp dried basil
1 l / 1 pint 16 fl. oz / 4 cups vegetable stock
100 g / 3 ½ oz / ½ cup crème fraiche
2 tbsp double (heavy) cream
2 tbsp extra virgin olive oil
a small handful of basil leaves, to garnish

METHOD

1. Heat the olive oil in a large saucepan set over a medium heat until hot.

2. Add the onion and celery; sweat with a little salt for 8–10 minutes until starting to brown.

3. Stir in the tomatoes, then add the dried basil and stock.

4. Stir well and bring to a simmer, then reduce the heat a little and cook for 20 minutes.

5. Blend the soup with a stick blender or in a food processor until smooth, then stir through the crème fraiche.

6. Return the soup to a simmer, then season to taste and ladle into bowls.

7. Garnish with a swirl of cream, a drizzle of extra virgin olive oil and a few basil leaves before serving.

TOP TIP
Pass the blended soup through a sieve and into a saucepan for an even texture.

Cream of Tomato Soup

SERVES 4

PREPARATION TIME **10–15 MINUTES**

COOKING TIME **40–45 MINUTES**

INGREDIENTS

tbsp olive oil

medium onion, finely chopped

sticks of celery, finely chopped

tsp caster (superfine) sugar

bay leaf

salt and freshly ground black pepper

g / 1 lb 10 oz / 5 cups ripe plum tomatoes,
blanched, deseeded and roughly chopped

ml / 1 pint 6 fl. oz / 3 cups vegetable
stock, hot

ml / 4 fl. oz / ½ cup double (heavy) cream

few sprigs of mint, finely chopped

few sprigs of flat-leaf parsley, finely chopped

METHOD

1. Heat the olive oil in a large saucepan set
   over a medium heat until hot.

2. Add the onion, celery, sugar, bay leaf and
   salt; sweat for 6–7 minutes until golden,
   then stir in the tomatoes.

3. Cover the saucepan with a lid and reduce the
   heat to low, allowing the tomatoes to stew
   for 10 minutes.

4. Add the stock to the saucepan. Stir well,
   then bring to a simmer and cook for
   20 minutes.

5. Discard the bay leaf, then blend the soup
   using a stick blender or food processor until
   smooth.

6. Stir through the double cream and return
   the soup to a simmer, then season to taste.

7. Ladle into bowls and garnish with a sprinkle
   of chopped herbs before serving.

TOP TIP

To prevent the soup
from splitting after
adding the cream,
don't let it boil.

13

Leek and Potato Soup

SERVES 4

PREPARATION TIME 10–15 MINUTES

COOKING TIME 30–35 MINUTES

INGREDIENTS

3 tbsp olive oil
1 large leek, sliced and washed
salt and freshly ground black pepper
350 g / 12 oz / 2 ⅓ cups floury potatoes,
    peeled and diced evenly
1 bay leaf
a few sprigs of thyme
1 l / 1 pint 12 fl. oz / 4 cups vegetable stock
75 g / 3 oz / ⅓ cup crème fraiche
100 g / 3 ½ oz / ½ cup of Brie, cut into 4 pieces

METHOD

1. Heat the olive oil in a large saucepan set over a medium heat until hot.

2. Sweat the leek with a little salt for 4–5 minutes, then add the potato. Continue to cook for 7–8 minutes until the potato starts to soften.

3. Add the bay leaf, thyme and stock. Stir well then bring to a simmer and cook for 20 minutes.

4. Discard the herbs, then blend the soup using a stick blender or food processor until smooth.

5. Stir through the crème fraiche and return the soup to a gentle simmer, then season to taste. Preheat the grill to hot.

6. Ladle the soup into bowls and top with a piece of Brie. Grill for 1–2 minutes until melted and golden.

7. Carefully remove the bowls from the grill and leave to stand for a minute before serving.

TOP TIP
Stir the potato from time to time as it sweats. This will prevent sticking.

Minestrone Soup

SERVES 4

PREPARATION TIME **10–15 MINUTES**

COOKING TIME **35–40 MINUTES**

INGREDIENTS

tbsp olive oil

rashers of back bacon, chopped

onion, finely chopped

medium carrots, peeled and diced

sticks of celery, diced

few sprigs of rosemary

g / 14 oz / 2 cups canned chopped tomatoes

l / 2 pints 4 fl. oz / 5 cups vegetable stock

g / 3 ½ oz / 1 cup ditalini pasta

and freshly ground black pepper

g / 2 oz / ½ cup Parmesan, grated

METHOD

1. Heat the olive oil in a large saucepan set over a medium heat until hot.

2. Add the bacon and sauté for 2–3 minutes, then add the onion, carrots, celery and rosemary, stirring well.

3. Cook for 6–7 minutes until the vegetables have softened slightly, then stir in the chopped tomatoes and stock.

4. Bring the soup to a simmer and cook over a reduced heat for 15 minutes until the vegetables are tender.

5. Add the ditalini pasta and simmer for 12–14 minutes until al dente.

6. Adjust the seasoning to taste, then ladle into bowls and garnish with some grated Parmesan and more freshly ground black pepper.

TOP TIP

Stir the soup after adding the pasta to prevent clumps forming.

French Onion Soup

SERVES **4**

PREPARATION TIME **10–15 MINUTES**

COOKING TIME **45–50 MINUTES**

INGREDIENTS

2 tbsp unsalted butter
1 tbsp olive oil
a few sprigs of thyme
1 bay leaf
2 cloves of garlic, crushed
7 medium brown onions, finely sliced
150 ml / 5 fl. oz / ⅔ cup dry white wine
1.25 l / 2 pints 4 fl. oz / 5 cups vegetable stock
salt and freshly ground black pepper
½ baguette, cut into thin slices
150 g / 5 oz / 1 ½ cups Gruyère, grated

METHOD

1. Melt the butter with the oil in a large, heavy-based saucepan set over a medium heat until hot.

2. Add the thyme, bay leaf, garlic and onions and sweat for 25–30 minutes, stirring occasionally, until lightly browned, then remove the herbs.

3. Deglaze the saucepan with white wine and let it reduce by half. Cover with the stock simmer for 15 minutes. Preheat the grill to hot.

4. Adjust the seasoning to taste and ladle into serving bowls.

5. Top with slices of baguette and a generous layer of Gruyère, then brown under the grill until the cheese is bubbling and golden in appearance.

6. Carefully remove from the grill before serving.

TOP TIP

Gradually sweat the onions. Cooking them 'low and slow' gives the best taste.

Carrot and Coriander Soup

SERVES 4

PREPARATION TIME **10–15 MINUTES**

COOKING TIME **30–35 MINUTES**

INGREDIENTS

tbsp olive oil

large onion, finely chopped

salt and freshly ground black pepper

tbsp ground coriander

750 g / 1 lb 10 oz / 5 cups carrots,
  peeled and chopped

1.5 l / 2 pints 4 fl. oz / 5 cups vegetable stock

tbsp fresh orange juice

small bunch of coriander (cilantro),
  roughly chopped

tbsp extra virgin olive oil, to garnish

METHOD

1. Heat the olive oil in a large saucepan set over a medium heat until hot.

2. Add the onion and sweat with a little salt for 4–5 minutes, stirring occasionally, until soft.

3. Add the ground coriander and stir well, cooking for a further minute. Add the carrots and stir well, then cover with the stock.

4. Bring to a simmer and cook steadily for 20–25 minutes until the carrot is soft but not mushy.

5. Blend with a stick blender or in a food processor, then return to a simmer in the saucepan.

6. Add orange juice to taste and season with salt and pepper.

7. Ladle into bowls and garnish with chopped coriander, a drizzle of extra virgin olive oil and some freshly ground black pepper before serving.

TOP TIP

When blending the soup, take care not to liquidise it. It should still retain its texture.

Creamy Mushroom Soup

SERVES **4**

PREPARATION TIME **10–15 MINUTES**

COOKING TIME **35–40 MINUTES**

INGREDIENTS

3 tbsp unsalted butter
225 g / 8 oz / 3 cups wild mushrooms, sliced
225 g / 8 oz / 3 cups white button
　　mushrooms, sliced
1 shallot, finely chopped
salt and freshly ground black pepper
1 l / 1 pint 16 fl. oz / 4 cups light chicken stock
1 bay leaf
125 ml / 4 ½ fl. oz / ½ cup double (heavy) cream
75 g / 3 oz / ¾ cup feta, crumbled

METHOD

1. Melt 2 tbsp of butter in a large saucepan set over a medium heat. Sauté the wild mushrooms, most of the button mushrooms and the shallot with seasoning until brown at the edges.

2. Add the stock and bay leaf, then stir well.

3. Bring the mixture to a simmer, then reduce the heat and cook for 25–30 minutes.

4. Discard the bay leaf and blend the mixture using a stick blender or food processor, then stir through the cream. Bring to a simmer and season to taste.

5. Heat the remaining butter in a small frying pan set over a moderate heat. Once lightly nutty in aroma, add the remaining sliced mushrooms and sauté until brown at the edges.

6. Ladle the soup into bowls and top with some sautéed mushrooms, feta and black pepper before serving.

TOP TIP

Make sure to account for the saltiness of the feta when seasoning this soup.

Pumpkin Soup

METHOD

1. Heat the olive oil in a large saucepan set over a medium heat until hot.

2. Sweat the onion and garlic with a little salt for 8–10 minutes, stirring occasionally until softened.

3. Add the dried sage and pumpkin, then stir well and cover with the stock.

4. Bring to a simmer, then reduce to a low heat and cook for 35–40 minutes until tender.

5. Blend using a stick blender or in a food processor until smooth, then return to a simmer.

6. Stir in the double cream until incorporated and adjust the seasoning to taste.

7. Ladle into soup bowls and garnish with a sprinkle of pumpkin seeds and a drizzle of herb or extra virgin olive oil.

8. Serve with any remaining pumpkin seeds in a bowl on the side.

RVES 4

EPARATION TIME **15 MINUTES**

OKING TIME **55–60 MINUTES**

GREDIENTS

ml / 2 fl. oz / ¼ cup olive oil

mall onions, finely diced

love of garlic, minced

t and freshly ground black pepper

sp dried sage

g / 2 lb 4 oz / 6 ½ cups pumpkin, peeled, deseeded and cut into even chunks

5 l / 2 pints 4 fl. oz / 5 cups vegetable stock

0 ml / 9 fl. oz / 1 cup double (heavy) cream

rb oil or extra virgin olive oil, to garnish

mall handful of pumpkin seeds

TOP TIP

Reduce the temperature of the soup to prevent the cream from splitting.

Carrot and Ginger Soup

SERVES 4

PREPARATION TIME **15 MINUTES**

COOKING TIME **35–40 MINUTES**

INGREDIENTS

3 tbsp unsalted butter
6 large carrots, peeled and diced
1 onion, finely chopped
salt and freshly ground black pepper
1 small orange, zest pared
2.5 cm (1 in) piece of root ginger,
    peeled and minced
500 ml / 18 fl. oz / 2 cups vegetable stock
500 ml / 18 fl. oz / 2 cups water
55 g / 2 oz / ½ cup Cheddar, grated
oatcakes or savoury biscuits, to serve

METHOD

1. Melt the butter in a large saucepan set over a medium heat until hot.

2. Add the carrot and onion; sweat with salt for 6–8 minutes until softened.

3. Stir in the orange zest and ginger, then cover with the stock and water.

4. Bring the liquid to a simmer, then cover and cook over a slightly reduced heat for 20 minutes.

5. Discard the orange zest, then blend the soup with a stick blender or food processor until smooth.

6. Bring the soup to a simmer, then season to taste.

7. Ladle into bowls and garnish with some grated Cheddar before serving with oatcakes or savoury biscuits.

TOP TIP

Cut the carrots into 2 ½ cm (1 in) cubes so that they cook evenly.

Roasted Parsnip Soup

RVES 4

EPARATION TIME **15 MINUTES**

OKING TIME **45–50 MINUTES**

GREDIENTS

osp olive oil

arge parsnips, peeled and evenly chopped

loves of garlic, minced

/ 1 pint 16 fl. oz / 4 cups vegetable stock

ml / 3 fl. oz / ⅓ cup whole (full-fat) milk

g / 3 oz / ¾ cup mimolette, shaved

osp hazelnuts (cobnuts), crushed

t and freshly ground black pepper

METHOD

1. Preheat the oven to 190°C (170°C fan) / 375F / gas 5 and grease and line a large baking tray with foil.

2. Toss together the olive oil, parsnips and garlic in a mixing bowl and spread out on the baking tray.

3. Roast for 20–25 minutes until golden at the edges, then remove from the oven and transfer to a large saucepan.

4. Cover with the stock and milk and bring to the boil over a moderate heat. Reduce the heat slightly, then cover and cook for 15 minutes.

5. Blend the soup with a stick blender or food processor until smooth. Return the soup to a simmer, then stir through some of the mimolette.

6. Season to taste, then ladle into bowls and garnish with the remaining mimolette and the crushed hazelnuts.

TOP TIP

Turn over the parsnips at least once as they roast to ensure even roasting.

Pepper Gazpacho

SERVES 4

PREPARATION TIME 10 MINUTES

INGREDIENTS

3 red peppers, deseeded and diced
1 tsp caster (superfine) sugar
1 red chilli (chili), deseeded and chopped
2 slices of white bread, crusts removed and diced
3 cloves of garlic, minced
400 g / 14 oz / 2 cups passata
400 g / 14 oz / 2 cups canned chopped tomatoes
2 tbsp sherry vinegar
75 ml / 3 fl. oz / ⅓ cup extra virgin olive oil
salt and freshly ground black pepper
2 tbsp sour cream
a few chives, snipped

METHOD

1. Blend the peppers in a food processor un
   finely chopped.

2. Add the sugar, chilli, bread, garlic, passa
   and chopped tomatoes and blend until smoc

3. Add some water to thin the consistency, i
   needed, then add the vinegar and olive oil

4. Pulse until combined, then season to tas
   before pouring into bowls.

5. Serve with a swirl of sour cream and
   some chives.

TOP TIP

Chill the gazpacho for 2 hours before serving to help develop its taste.

weet Potato oup

SERVES 4

PREPARATION TIME 10–15 MINUTES

COOKING TIME 25 MINUTES

INGREDIENTS

sp sunflower oil

spring onions (scallions), chopped

and freshly ground black pepper

sp ground cumin

sp ground coriander

nch of Cayenne pepper

g / 1 lb 10 oz / 5 cups sweet potatoes,
peeled and grated

1 pint 16 fl. oz / 4 cups vegetable stock

ml / 4 ½ fl. oz / ½ cup double (heavy) cream

nall handful of coriander (cilantro) leaves,
o garnish

METHOD

1. Heat the oil in a large saucepan set over a medium heat until hot. Add the spring onions and sweat with a little salt for 3 minutes, stirring occasionally.

2. Add the ground spices and cook for 1 minute, then stir in the grated sweet potato.

3. Cover with the stock and bring to a simmer; cook steadily for 6–8 minutes until the sweet potato is tender.

4. Blend using a stick blender or in a food processor until smooth, then return to a simmer over a medium heat.

5. Add the cream and stir well. Season to taste with salt and pepper.

6. Ladle into bowls and garnish with coriander leaves before serving.

TOP TIP

Cook the spices over a medium heat or lower to avoid burning.

Split Pea Soup

SERVES 4

PREPARATION TIME **10–15 MINUTES**

COOKING TIME **45–55 MINUTES**

INGREDIENTS

2 tbsp unsalted butter
1 medium onion, finely chopped
1 bay leaf
salt and freshly ground black pepper
150 g / 5 oz / ⅔ cup split peas, soaked in water
    overnight and drained
1.25 l / 2 pints 4 fl. oz / 5 cups vegetable stock
225 g / 8 oz / 2 cups frozen peas
75 ml / 3 fl. oz / ⅓ cup whole (full-fat) milk
55 ml / 2 fl. oz / ¼ cup double (heavy) cream
a few sprigs of dill, to garnish

METHOD

1. Melt the butter in a large saucepan set over a medium heat until hot.

2. Add the onion, bay leaf and a little salt. Sweat for 4–5 minutes until softened, then add the drained split peas and stock.

3. Bring to the boil, then reduce to a simmer and cook for 40–50 minutes until tender.

4. Discard the bay leaf, then add the frozen peas and milk. Simmer for 2 minutes, then blend with a stick blender or in a food processor until smooth.

5. Return the soup to a simmer and season to taste.

6. Ladle into bowls, swirl through a little cream and serve with a garnish of dill on top.

TOP TIP

Simmer the soup for an hour over a low heat until the peas are soft enough to purée.

Beetroot and Rhubarb Soup

RVES 4

EPARATION TIME **10 MINUTES**

OKING TIME **20–25 MINUTES**

GREDIENTS

tbsp olive oil

ion, finely chopped

rge stick of rhubarb, trimmed and diced

ay leaf

t and freshly ground black pepper

g / 1 lb 2 oz / 3 ⅓ cups cooked beetroot in
juice, drained and thinly sliced

g / 7 oz / 1 cup passata

ml / 18 fl. oz / 2 cups vegetable stock

sp cumin seeds, to garnish

sp Greek yogurt

METHOD

1. Heat the olive oil in a large saucepan set
   over a medium heat until hot.

2. Add the onion, rhubarb, bay leaf and salt,
   then sweat for 6–7 minutes until softened.

3. Stir in most of the beetroot, then cover with
   the passata and stock. Bring to a simmer
   and cook gently for 8–10 minutes, then
   remove the bay leaf.

4. Blend the soup using a stick blender or in a
   food processor until smooth, then return to
   a simmer and season to taste.

5. Ladle the soup into bowls and garnish with
   the remaining beetroot, a pinch of cumin
   seeds and a swirl of Greek yogurt.

TOP TIP

Use cooked beetroot in
natural juices rather
than beetroot in
vinegar.

Spinach and Fennel Soup

SERVES 4

PREPARATION TIME 10 MINUTES

COOKING TIME 25–30 MINUTES

INGREDIENTS

2 tbsp unsalted butter
1 tbsp olive oil
1 large onion, finely chopped
2 medium fennel bulbs, fronds trimmed and
    finely sliced
salt and freshly ground black pepper
3 large white potatoes, peeled and sliced
1 l / 1 pint 16 fl. oz / 4 cups vegetable stock
110 ml / 4 fl. oz / ½ cup whole (full-fat) milk
150 g / 5 oz / 3 cups baby spinach, washed
½ tsp paprika, to garnish

METHOD

1. Melt the butter with the oil in a large saucepan set over a medium heat until ho

2. Add the onion, sliced fennel and a little sa and sweat for 5–6 minutes, then add the potato.

3. Continue to cook for 4–5 minutes, stirring frequently, then cover with the stock and milk.

4. Bring to a simmer and cook for 15 minute until the potato is soft, then stir through h of the spinach and cook for a further minu

5. Remove some of the potato slices from th pan and blend the rest of the soup with a stick blender or in a food processor until smooth.

6. Return the soup to a simmer, then add the rest of the spinach and the reserved potato slices.

7. Season to taste, then ladle into bowls and serve with a pinch of paprika.

TOP TIP

To preserve the taste of the spinach, cook it for just 1 minute before blending.

Asparagus Soup

RVES 4

EPARATION TIME **10–15 MINUTES**

OKING TIME **25 MINUTES**

GREDIENTS

- 0 g / 1 lb / 4 cups asparagus,
  woody ends removed
- sp olive oil
- medium onion, finely chopped
- ticks of celery, finely diced
- love of garlic, minced
- t and freshly ground black pepper
- / 1 pint 16 fl. oz / 4 cups vegetable stock
- sp unsalted butter
- 0 g / 3 ½ oz / 1 cup goats' cheese, to serve

METHOD

1. Cut off the tips from the asparagus and reserve, then roughly chop the stalks.

2. Heat the olive oil in a large saucepan set over a medium heat until hot.

3. Add the onion, celery, garlic and a little salt.

4. Sweat for 5–6 minutes, then add the chopped asparagus stalks.

5. Cover with the stock, stir well and simmer for 15 minutes, then stir through the butter.

6. Blend the soup using a stick blender or in a food processor until smooth, then return the soup to a simmer and season to taste.

7. Blanch the asparagus tips in a saucepan of salted, boiling water for 1 minute, then drain.

8. Ladle the soup into bowls and garnish with goats' cheese and the asparagus tips, then serve.

TOP TIP

Refresh the asparagus tips in a bowl of iced water after blanching and draining.

41

Minted Pea Soup

SERVES **4**

PREPARATION TIME **10 MINUTES**

COOKING TIME **15 MINUTES**

INGREDIENTS

2 tbsp olive oil
2 spring onions (scallions), chopped
1 clove of garlic, minced
salt and freshly ground black pepper
300 g / 10 ½ oz / 3 cups frozen peas, thawed
1 l / 1 pint 16 fl. oz / 4 cups vegetable stock
1 small bunch of mint, leaves picked
1 tbsp lemon juice
rice crackers, to serve

METHOD

1. Heat the olive oil in a large saucepan set over a medium heat until hot.

2. Add the spring onion, garlic and a little salt and sweat for 4–5 minutes, stirring frequently.

3. Add the peas, stock and most of the mint leaves, stirring well.

4. Bring to a simmer and cook for 5 minutes, then blend with a stick blender or in a food processor until smooth.

5. Return to a simmer and season with lemon juice, salt and pepper as needed.

6. Ladle into bowls and garnish with the remaining mint leaves. Serve with rice crackers on the side.

TOP TIP

As a substitute for fresh mint, stir in 2 tsp of dried mint, then blend the soup.

Broccoli and Stilton Broth

METHOD

1. Melt the butter with the oil in a large saucepan set over a medium heat until hot.

2. Add the onion, celery and a little salt and sweat for 5–6 minutes, stirring occasionally.

3. Add the broccoli and most of the lettuce, then cover with the stock.

4. Stir well and bring to a simmer. Cook for 15–20 minutes until the broccoli is tender.

5. Add the Stilton and blend the soup with a stick blender or in a food processor until smooth.

6. Return the soup to a simmer and season to taste.

7. Ladle into bowls and garnish with 1 tbsp of ricotta and the remaining lettuce. Serve with baguette toasts on the side.

RVES 4

EPARATION TIME **10–15 MINUTES**

OKING TIME **25–30 MINUTES**

GREDIENTS

sp unsalted butter

sp sunflower oil

rge onion, finely chopped

ick of celery, finely chopped

t and freshly ground black pepper

rge head of broccoli, evenly chopped

em lettuce, chopped

1 pint 16 fl. oz / 4 cups vegetable stock

g / 5 oz / 1 ½ cups good-quality Stilton

g / 2 oz / ¼ cup ricotta, to serve

uette toasts, to serve

TOP TIP

Use a dollop of crème fraiche or Greek yogurt instead of the ricotta.

Meat Soups

Chicken and Lemon Broth

SERVES 4

PREPARATION TIME **10 MINUTES**

COOKING TIME **25 MINUTES**

INGREDIENTS

2 tbsp sunflower oil

2 shallots, sliced

salt and freshly ground black pepper

2 large skinless chicken breasts, sliced

150 g / 5 oz / 1 cup cooked long grain rice

250 ml / 9 fl. oz / 1 cup coconut milk

1 l / 1 pint 16 fl. oz / 4 cups chicken stock

1 lemon, juiced and finely zested

2 tbsp rice wine vinegar

1 tbsp fish sauce

1 tsp caster (superfine) sugar

a small handful of chive stalks, chopped

METHOD

1. Heat the oil in a large saucepan set over a medium heat until hot.

2. Add the shallot and a little salt. Sweat for 2–3 minutes, then add the chicken and rice.

3. Stir well and cook for 2–3 minutes. Cover with the coconut milk, stock and lemon juice.

4. Bring to a simmer and cook steadily for 12–15 minutes until the chicken is cooked through.

5. Season to taste with rice wine vinegar, fish sauce, sugar and pepper before stirring through the lemon zest.

6. Ladle into bowls and garnish with chives before serving.

TOP TIP

A microplane is ideal for finely zesting the lemon in this recipe.

reamy hicken Soup

VES **4**

PARATION TIME **10 MINUTES**

KING TIME **30 MINUTES**

REDIENTS

sp unsalted butter
on, finely chopped
k, washed and sliced
ge carrots, peeled and roughly sliced
and freshly ground black pepper
ge skinless chicken breasts
1 pint 16 fl. oz / 4 cups chicken stock
ml / 4 fl. oz / ½ cup double (heavy) cream
g / 5 oz / 1 ½ cups asparagus,
oody ends removed
g / 3 ½ oz / 1 cup frozen peas
v sprigs of chervil, to garnish

METHOD

1. Melt the butter in a large saucepan set over a medium heat until hot.

2. Add the onion, leek, carrots and a little salt and sweat for 5–6 minutes, stirring occasionally.

3. Add the chicken breasts and stock. Bring to a simmer and cook for 20 minutes until the chicken is cooked through.

4. Remove the chicken from the soup and set to one side, then add the cream and return the soup to a simmer.

5. Add the asparagus spears and let them cook for 2 minutes before adding the peas and simmering for a further 2 minutes.

6. Slice the chicken and stir the pieces back into the soup. Adjust the seasoning to taste.

7. Ladle into bowls and garnish with chervil sprigs before serving.

TOP TIP

When the chicken is simmering in the broth, skim away any excess residue.

Chicken and Vegetable Soup

SERVES 4

PREPARATION TIME 10–15 MINUTES

COOKING TIME 30–35 MINUTES

INGREDIENTS

2 tbsp sesame oil
salt and freshly ground black pepper
2 large chicken breasts, trimmed
1 red chilli (chili), sliced
1 shallot, finely chopped
1.25 l / 2 pints 4 fl. oz / 5 cups chicken stock
150 g / 5 oz / 2 cups mushrooms, chopped
200 g / 7 oz / 1 cup canned sweetcorn, drained
1 large egg, beaten
1 tbsp dark soy sauce
1 tbsp rice wine vinegar
a small bunch of coriander (cilantro),
    roughly chopped

METHOD

1. Heat the sesame oil in a large saucepan
   over a moderate heat until hot. Season the
   chicken breasts and seal in the oil until the
   skin is golden.

2. Remove from the pan and reduce the heat a
   little, then add the chilli and shallot.

3. Sauté for 2 minutes, then cover with the
   stock. Return the chicken breasts to the pan
   along with the mushrooms and sweetcorn.

4. Bring to a simmer and cook steadily for
   15–18 minutes until the chicken breasts are
   cooked through.

5. Remove the chicken and slice, then return to
   the saucepan. Stir through the beaten egg
   and cook for a further 2 minutes, then
   season to taste with soy sauce, rice wine
   vinegar, salt and pepper.

6. Stir through the chopped coriander before
   ladling into bowls and serving.

TOP TIP

After adding the egg, continue to stir so it is evenly distributed through the soup.

Pea and Ham Soup

SERVES 4

PREPARATION TIME **10 MINUTES**

COOKING TIME **25 MINUTES**

INGREDIENTS

- tbsp unsalted butter
- onion, finely chopped
- medium white potato, peeled and diced
- 0 g / 9 oz / 1 ⅔ cups cooked gammon steak
- ml 16 fl. oz / 4 cups ham stock
- 0 g / 1 lb / 4 cups frozen peas
- ml / 4 fl. oz / ½ cup whole (full-fat) milk
- t and freshly ground black pepper

METHOD

1. Melt the butter in a large saucepan set over a medium heat until hot.

2. Add the onion, potato and a little salt; sweat for 5-6 minutes, stirring occasionally.

3. Add the gammon and the stock. Bring to a simmer over a moderate heat, then cook steadily for 15 minutes until the potato is very tender.

4. Remove the gammon steak and set to one side to cool. Add the peas to the soup and simmer for 2 minutes.

5. Blend the soup with a stick blender or in a food processor until smooth, then return to a simmer and stir through the milk.

6. Season to taste before ladling into bowls. Shred the gammon steak between a couple of forks and serve on top of the soup with a little more pepper.

TOP TIP

Adjust the amount of milk you add to thin out the soup to the desired consistency.

Ham and Cabbage Broth

SERVES 4

PREPARATION TIME 10–15 MINUTES

COOKING TIME 25 MINUTES

INGREDIENTS

1 large Savoy cabbage, leaves separated
100 g / 3 ½ oz / ⅔ cup pancetta lardons
1 onion, finely chopped
1 l / 1 pint 16 fl. oz / 4 cups chicken or ham stock
a small handful of sage sprigs
salt and freshly ground black pepper
1 tbsp lemon juice

METHOD

1. Using a sharp knife, remove the centre stalks from the cabbage leaves, then fine slice the leaves and set to one side.

2. Heat a large saucepan over a medium heat until hot, then add the pancetta and fry for 3–4 minutes until golden.

3. Remove half of the pancetta and drain on kitchen paper. Add the sliced cabbage and onion and sweat for 2 minutes.

4. Cover with the stock and bring to a simmer, then cook for 15 minutes until the cabbage is tender.

5. Stir through the sage and season to taste with salt, pepper and lemon juice.

6. Ladle into bowls and garnish with the reserved pancetta on top.

TOP TIP
To garnish the dish, cook the pancetta under a hot grill or reheat in a microwave.

Leek and Bacon Soup

SERVES 4

PREPARATION TIME **10–15 MINUTES**

COOKING TIME **20–25 MINUTES**

INGREDIENTS

- tbsp unsalted butter
- tbsp olive oil
- rashers of streaky bacon, sliced
- large leeks, washed and sliced
- medium white potatoes, peeled and diced evenly
- salt and freshly ground black pepper
- 1 pint 16 fl. oz / 4 cups vegetable or ham stock
- pinch of crushed red peppercorns

METHOD

1. Melt the butter with the olive oil in a large saucepan set over a medium heat until hot.

2. Add the bacon and sauté for 2 minutes, then add the leek, potato and a little salt.

3. Continue to cook for 4–5 minutes, stirring occasionally, then cover with the stock.

4. Bring to a simmer and cook for 15–20 minutes until the potato is tender.

5. Season to taste, then ladle into bowls. Garnish with a pinch of the crushed red peppercorns and some freshly ground black pepper before serving.

TOP TIP

To enhance the taste of the bacon, use ham stock rather than vegetable.

Lentil and Bacon Soup

SERVES 4

PREPARATION TIME **10 MINUTES**

COOKING TIME **30–35 MINUTES**

INGREDIENTS

2 tbsp sunflower oil
1 onion, finely chopped
1 clove of garlic, minced
1 bay leaf
salt and freshly ground black pepper
½ tsp ground cumin
250 g / 9 oz / 1 cup red lentils
1.25 l / 2 pints 4 fl. oz / 5 cups vegetable or
   ham stock
4 rashers of streaky bacon
a pinch of Cayenne pepper

METHOD

1. Heat the oil in a large saucepan set over a
   medium heat until hot. Add the onion, garlic,
   bay leaf and a little salt and sweat for
   5 minutes.

2. Add the ground cumin, then stir in the
   lentils. Cover with the stock and bring to a
   boil for 5 minutes.

3. Reduce to a simmer for 20–25 minutes until
   the lentils have absorbed the stock and are
   tender. Preheat the grill to hot.

4. Discard the bay leaf and blend the soup
   using a stick blender or a food processor
   until smooth. Return to a simmer in
   the saucepan.

5. Season to taste and keep warm over a low
   heat. Grill the bacon for 4–5 minutes,
   turning once, until golden and crispy.

6. Ladle the soup into mugs or bowls and top
   with rashers of bacon and a pinch of
   Cayenne before serving.

TOP TIP

When boiling the lentils, use a large spoon to remove any residue from the surface.

omato and horizo Soup

METHOD

1. Heat the oil in a large saucepan set over a medium heat until hot.

2. Add the bay leaf, celery, garlic and a little salt. Sauté for 2 minutes, then add the chorizo.

3. Continue to cook for 3 minutes, stirring occasionally, then add the paprika, cherry tomatoes, passata and lentils.

4. Stir well, then cover with the stock and bring to the boil. Cook for 5 minutes, then reduce to a gentle simmer for 20 minutes until the lentils are tender.

5. Adjust the seasoning to taste, ladle into bowls and serve.

:VES 4

PARATION TIME 10–15 MINUTES

KING TIME 30 MINUTES

REDIENTS

sp olive oil

y leaf

cks of celery, sliced

ves of garlic, minced

and freshly ground black pepper

g / 5 oz / 1 cup chorizo, peeled and sliced

smoked paprika

g / 5 oz / 1 cup cherry tomatoes, halved

g / 7 oz / 1 cup passata

g / 3 ½ oz / ⅔ cup yellow split lentils, rinsed

l / 2 pints 4 fl. oz / 5 cups vegetable stock

TOP TIP

Make sure to rinse the lentils really well to get rid of any grit and dirt.

Sausage and Bean Soup

SERVES **4**

PREPARATION TIME **10–15 MINUTES**

COOKING TIME **35–40 MINUTES**

INGREDIENTS

2 tbsp olive oil

2 small onions, roughly chopped

1 clove of garlic, chopped

½ red pepper, deseeded and diced

1 medium courgette (zucchini), deseeded, peeled and finely diced

salt and freshly ground black pepper

4 thick, good-quality sausages

400 g / 14 oz / 2 cups canned cannellini beans, drained

a few sprigs of thyme

125 ml / 4 ½ fl. oz / ½ cup cider

1 l / 1 pint 16 fl. oz / 4 cups ham stock

METHOD

1. Heat the olive oil in a large saucepan set over a medium heat until hot.

2. Add the onion, garlic, pepper, courgette and a little salt and sweat for 5–6 minute until softened.

3. Prick the sausages with a fork, then cut them in half and add them to the pan. Cook until browned, then add the beans and thyme.

4. Stir well, then increase the heat and add cider; let it reduce by half before pouring the stock.

5. Bring the soup to a simmer and cook gen for 25–30 minutes until the sausages are cooked through.

6. Adjust the seasoning to taste, then ladle bowls and serve.

TOP TIP
To substitute the cider, use a splash of apple juice when adding the stock.

xtail and Vegetable oup

RVES 4

PARATION TIME **15 MINUTES**

KING TIME **1 HOUR 5–10 MINUTES**

GREDIENTS

sp sunflower oil
and freshly ground black pepper
g / 9 oz / 1 ⅔ cups oxtail
ge onions, finely chopped
cks of celery, finely chopped
ge carrots, peeled and finely diced
ge courgette (zucchini), finely diced
l / 2 pints 4 fl. oz / 5 cups vegetable stock
ml / 9 fl. oz / 1 cup double (heavy) cream
hall handful of flat-leaf parsley,
oughly chopped

METHOD

1. Heat the oil in a large saucepan set over a moderate heat until hot. Season the oxtail and brown in the oil, then remove to one side.

2. Reduce the heat slightly, then add the onion and most of the celery, carrot and courgette, retaining some as a garnish.

3. Sweat for 4–5 minutes, stirring occasionally, before returning the oxtail and covering with the stock.

4. Bring to a simmer and cook gently for 45–50 minutes.

5. Remove the oxtail and blend the soup using a stick blender or in a food processor, then return to the saucepan and add the cream.

6. Bring the soup to a simmer and season to taste. Ladle into bowls.

7. Shred the oxtail meat and serve on top with the reserved vegetable garnish and some parsley.

TOP TIP

To thicken, whisk in 1 tbsp of cornflour (cornstarch) and a splash of water.

67

Fish Soups

Smoked Haddock Chowder

SERVES 4

PREPARATION TIME **15 MINUTES**

COOKING TIME **30 MINUTES**

INGREDIENTS

450 g / 1 lb / 3 cups smoked haddock fillets
(un-dyed)
1 l / 1 pint 16 fl. oz / 4 cups whole (full-fat) milk
2 tbsp unsalted butter
2 onions, finely chopped
2 sticks of celery, sliced
2 large white potatoes, peeled and diced
1 bay leaf
75 ml / 3 fl. oz / ⅓ cup double (heavy) cream
cream crackers, to serve
1 lemon, cut into wedges
salt and freshly ground black pepper

METHOD

1. Place the haddock in a large saucepan and
   cover with the milk. Bring to a simmer over
   a moderate heat and leave for 2 minutes.

2. Turn off the heat and cover the saucepan
   with a lid, then leave to cool for 5 minutes.

3. Remove the haddock and flake into large
   chunks, discarding any skin and bones.
   Reserve the milk.

4. Melt the butter in another large saucepan
   set over a medium heat until hot, then add
   the onion, half the celery and the potato.

5. Cook for 4–5 minutes, stirring occasionally
   then add the bay leaf and cover with the
   reserved milk.

6. Bring to a simmer and cook for 15 minutes
   until the potato is tender. Remove some of
   the potato and the bay leaf. Blend until
   smooth using a stick blender or in a
   food processor.

7. Return the soup to a simmer and stir
   through the cream, reserved potato,
   haddock and celery. Season to taste.
   Serve with crackers and lemon wedges.

TOP TIP

Remove all the bones, cartilage and skin from the haddock fillets.

obster isque

VES **4**

PARATION TIME **15 MINUTES**

KING TIME **40 MINUTES**

GREDIENTS

- 75 g / 1 lb 8 oz lobster, placed in the freezer or 2 hours beforehand
- sp unsalted butter
- allots, finely chopped
- cks of celery, chopped
- ve of garlic, minced
- and freshly ground black pepper
- sp sherry or brandy
- sp tomato purée
- 1 pint 16 fl. oz / 4 cups fish stock
- w sprigs of tarragon, finely chopped
- w sprigs of oregano, to garnish
- atta slices, to serve

METHOD

1. Bring a large saucepan of salted water to the boil. Plunge the lobster into the water and cover with a lid, cooking for 15 minutes.

2. Remove the cooked lobster with a pair of tongs and rinse under cold water for 1 minute. Leave to cool.

3. Melt the butter in a large saucepan set over a medium heat until hot. Add the shallot, celery, garlic and a little salt. Sweat for 5–6 minutes.

4. Add the sherry or brandy and leave to reduce slightly before stirring in the tomato purée and stock.

5. Bring to a simmer and cook for 15 minutes, then add the tarragon and blend with a stick blender or in a food processor until smooth.

6. Return to a simmer and season to taste. Separate the lobster and crack the claws and shell to extract the meat.

7. Ladle the bisque into bowls and top with the lobster. Garnish with oregano and serve with slices of ciabatta.

TOP TIP

Simmer the shell of the lobster for 10 minutes before adding to the bisque.

Mussel Chowder

SERVES **4**

PREPARATION TIME **15–20 MINUTES**

COOKING TIME **40–45 MINUTES**

INGREDIENTS

2 tbsp unsalted butter

2 shallots, finely chopped

2 cloves of garlic, minced

100 g / 3 ½ oz / ⅔ cup pancetta, diced

1 bay leaf

a few sprigs of thyme

600 g / 1 lb 5 oz / 4 cups floury potatoes,
    peeled and cubed

1.2 l / 2 pints / 5 cups fish stock, hot

150 ml / 5 fl. oz / ⅔ cup double (heavy) cream

600 g / 1 lb 5 oz / 4 cups mussels, cleaned with
    beards removed

175 ml / 6 fl. oz / ¾ cup dry white wine

a small handful of flat-leaf parsley,
    finely chopped

salt and freshly ground black pepper

METHOD

1. Melt the butter in a large saucepan set ov
    a medium heat until hot.

2. Sweat the shallot, garlic, pancetta, bay le
    and thyme for 5–6 minutes, stirring
    occasionally. Add the potato and continue
    to cook for 4–5 minutes.

3. Cover with the stock, then bring to a simm
    and cook for 15–20 minutes. Discard the
    herbs and blend with a stick blender or in
    food processor until smooth.

4. Return the chowder to a simmer, then stir
    through the cream.

5. Meanwhile, heat another large saucepan
    over a moderate heat until hot. Add the
    mussels and wine, cover with a lid and lea
    the mussels to cook for 3–4 minutes
    until opened.

6. Drain the mussels and discard any that
    haven't opened.

7. Remove the meat from the shells and stir
    three-quarters into the chowder.

8. Ladle the chowder into bowls and top with
    the remaining mussels and a sprinkling c
    parsley before serving.

TOP TIP

Before cooking, discard any open mussels as these are not safe to eat.

eafood Broth

REDIENTS

sp olive oil
cks of celery, sliced
edium carrot, peeled and sliced
nnel bulb, sliced, with fronds reserved
and freshly ground black pepper
g / 5 oz / 1 cup mussels, cleaned with
eards removed
g / 5 oz / 1 cup clams, rinsed
g / 8 oz / 1 ½ cups whole prawns
shrimp), deveined
l / 2 pints 4 fl. oz / 5 cups fish stock
g / 5 oz / 1 cup skinless cod or haddock fillet,
ut into chunks
sp lemon juice
d chilli (chili), deseeded and finely chopped

METHOD

1. Heat the olive oil in a large saucepan set over a medium heat until hot.

2. Add the celery, carrot, fennel and a little salt. Sweat for 6–7 minutes, stirring occasionally, until softened.

3. Add the mussels, clams and prawns to the saucepan, then cover with the stock.

4. Bring to a simmer, cover with a lid, and cook for 7–8 minutes, until the clams and mussels have opened. Discard any that don't.

5. Add the chunks of fish and cook, uncovered, for 4–5 minutes until they are cooked through.

6. Season to taste with lemon juice, salt and pepper before ladling into dishes.

7. Serve with a garnish of fennel fronds and a sprinkle of red chilli on top.

TOP TIP

Soften the vegetables without browning, as this will preserve the seafood taste.

Chunky Fish Soup

SERVES 4

PREPARATION TIME 15 MINUTES

COOKING TIME 25–30 MINUTES

INGREDIENTS

2 tbsp olive oil

1 large onion, finely sliced

2 cloves of garlic, minced

salt and freshly ground black pepper

1 tbsp tomato purée

2 tbsp brandy

200 g / 7 oz / 1 cup canned chopped tomatoes

1 l / 1 pint 16 fl. oz / 4 cups fish stock

300 g / 10 ½ oz / 2 cups mussels, cleaned with beards removed

225 g / 8 oz / 1 ½ cups whole prawns (shrimp), peeled and deveined with tails intact

300 g / 10 ½ oz / 2 cups skinless cod fillet, cut into chunks

a small handful of basil leaves

METHOD

1. Heat the olive oil in a large saucepan set over a medium heat until hot.

2. Add the onion, garlic and a little salt. Sweat for 5–6 minutes, stirring occasion

3. Stir in the tomato purée and brandy. Cook for 1 minute, then cover with the chopped tomatoes and stock.

4. Bring to a simmer and cook for 10 minut then add the mussels and prawns. Cover with a lid and cook for 4 minutes, then stir in the cod.

5. Simmer, uncovered, for another 4 minut and season to taste.

6. Ladle into bowls and garnish with basil leaves before serving.

TOP TIP

For a thick soup, blend with a stick blender before adding the seafood.

lam Chowder

PARATION TIME **15 MINUTES**

KING TIME **30 MINUTES**

REDIENTS

p unsalted butter
hers of back bacon, chopped
dium onion, finely chopped
ks of celery, chopped
p plain (all-purpose) flour
ml / 1 pint 3 fl. oz / 2 ½ cups chicken stock
/ 1 lb / 3 cups floury potatoes,
eled and diced
ge carrot, diced
/ 1 lb / 3 cups assorted clams, rinsed
ml / 6 fl. oz / ¾ cup double (heavy) cream
and freshly ground black pepper
sprigs of thyme, to garnish

METHOD

1. Melt the butter in a large saucepan set over a medium heat until hot.

2. Add the bacon, onion and celery. Sauté for 4–5 minutes, stirring occasionally, then sprinkle over the flour.

3. Stir well and slowly whisk in the stock. Bring the chowder to a simmer, then add the potato and carrot.

4. Cover with a lid and cook over a reduced heat for 15 minutes until the potato and carrot are tender.

5. Add the clams, cover with a lid, and continue to cook for a further 5 minutes until they have opened. Discard any that don't.

6. Add the cream and bring to a simmer for a few minutes before seasoning to taste.

7. Ladle into bowls and serve with a garnish of thyme on top.

TOP TIP
Slowly incorporate the stock with a whisk to avoid lumps in your chowder.

Crab Soup

SERVES 4

PREPARATION TIME 10–15 MINUTES

COOKING TIME 20–25 MINUTES

INGREDIENTS

1 tbsp sunflower oil
2 spring onions (scallions), finely chopped
2 cm (1 in) piece of root ginger, peeled and grated
1 l / 1 pint 16 fl. oz / 4 cups chicken stock
1 x 675 g / 1 lb 8 oz crab
1 tbsp cornflour (cornstarch)
1 tbsp rice wine
1 tbsp rice wine vinegar
salt and freshly ground black pepper
1 large egg, beaten
2 pak choi, chopped
a small handful of watercress

METHOD

1. Heat the oil in a large saucepan set over medium heat until hot. Add the spring o and ginger. Sweat for 3–4 minutes, then cover with the stock.

2. Bring to the boil before carefully loweri the crab into the saucepan. Cook at a simmer for 8–9 minutes, then carefully remove with a pair of tongs.

3. Return the liquid to a simmer and whisk together the cornflour with 1 tbsp of wat Whisk the paste into the broth before seasoning with the rice wine, rice wine vinegar, salt and pepper.

4. Whisk in the beaten egg and pak choi. Tu off the heat and cook the pak choi and eg

5. Remove the claws from the crab as well the legs and purse. Discard the dead ma fingers, then crack the shells and extra much meat as you can.

6. Ladle the soup into bowls and add the crabmeat. Garnish with watercress before serving.

TOP TIP

Wrap the cooked crab in a towel or cloth before cracking the shell with a hammer.

Salt Cod Soup

METHOD

1. Heat the olive oil in a large saucepan set over a medium heat until hot.

2. Add the onion, celery, garlic and a little salt and sweat for 5–6 minutes, stirring occasionally, until softened.

3. Add the salt cod to the saucepan as well as the broccoli and stock, then bring to a simmer and cook for 15–20 minutes until the broccoli is tender.

4. Stir through the parsley and adjust the seasoning to taste before ladling into serving bowls.

RVES 4

EPARATION TIME **10 MINUTES**

OKING TIME **25–30 MINUTES**

GREDIENTS

bsp olive oil

nion, finely chopped

ticks of celery, finely chopped

oves of garlic, minced

t and freshly ground black pepper

0 g / 12 oz / 2 ⅓ cups salt cod, soaked in cold water overnight and drained

arge head of broccoli, prepared into florets

/ 1 pint 16 fl. oz / 4 cups vegetable stock

mall handful of flat-leaf parsley, finely chopped

TOP TIP

Use salt sparingly, as the cod will retain some salt, even after soaking overnight.

Exotic, Spicy and Noodle Soups

Mushroom and Foie Gras Soup

SERVES 4

PREPARATION TIME **10–15 MINUTES**

COOKING TIME **25–30 MINUTES**

INGREDIENTS

2 tbsp olive oil
1 shallot, finely chopped
salt and freshly ground back pepper
150 g / 5 oz / 2 cups mixed wild mushrooms
1.25 l / 2 pints 4 fl. oz / 5 cups beef stock
250 g / 9 oz / 1 ⅔ cups foie gras, deveined
150 g / 5 oz / 1 ½ cups broad (fava) beans, shelled
a small handful of flat-leaf parsley,
    finely chopped
a small handful of chive stalks

METHOD

1. Heat the oil in a large saucepan set over medium heat until hot.

2. Add the shallot and a little salt. Sweat for 3–4 minutes, then add the mixed wild mushrooms.

3. Cook for 2–3 minutes, stirring occasionally, then cover with the stock. Bring to a simmer and cook for 10–15 minutes until the mushrooms are tender.

4. Heat a frying pan over a moderate heat until hot. Season the foie gras and sear in the pan until golden. Remove from the pan and drain on kitchen paper, then slice.

5. Stir the sliced foie gras into the soup along with the broad beans and chopped parsley. Leave to warm through for a couple of minutes.

6. Finely chop a few chive stalks and stir into the soup. Season to taste with salt and pepper.

7. Ladle into bowls and garnish with the remaining chive stalks before serving.

TOP TIP

A pair of kitchen tweezers will help when deveining the foie gras.

...hai Coconut
...oup

METHOD

1. Combine the stock, coconut milk, fish sauce, rice wine vinegar and sugar in a large saucepan set over a medium heat and whisk well.

2. Bring to a simmer before adding the chicken. Cook the chicken at a gentle simmer for 15 minutes, then add the courgette and spring onion.

3. Stir well and cook gently for a further 5–7 minutes until the courgette is soft.

4. Season to taste with lime juice, salt and pepper before ladling into bowls.

5. Garnish with coriander before serving.

...ES **4**

...RATION TIME **10–15 MINUTES**

...NG TIME **25 MINUTES**

...REDIENTS

...l / 18 fl. oz / 2 cups chicken stock
...l / 18 fl. oz / 2 cups coconut milk
... fish sauce
... rice wine vinegar
...e pinch of soft, light brown sugar
...e skinless chicken breasts, sliced
...ium courgette (zucchini),
...seeded and diced
...ng onions (scallions), finely sliced
...e, juiced
...nd freshly ground black pepper
...l bunch of coriander (cilantro),
...ughly chopped

TOP TIP
Instead of adding more salt to season the soup, try adding a dash of fish sauce.

Chicken Miso Soup

SERVES **4**

PREPARATION TIME **10 MINUTES**

COOKING TIME **35 MINUTES**

INGREDIENTS

2 tbsp sesame oil
1 tbsp white miso paste
1 l / 1 pint 16 fl. oz / 4 cups chicken stock
2 small skinless chicken breasts
200 g / 7 oz / 2 cups udon noodles
1 pak choi, sliced
2 spring onions (scallions), finely sliced
salt and freshly ground black pepper
a pinch of red chilli (chili) flakes

METHOD

1. Heat the sesame oil in a large saucepan over a medium heat until hot.

2. Whisk in the miso paste and follow with stock immediately after.

3. Add the chicken breasts and cook at a simmer for 20 minutes, then remove from the broth and leave to cool.

4. Add the noodles to the broth and simmer steadily for 10–12 minutes until soft. Meanwhile, shred the chicken breasts before stirring them back into the broth.

5. Add the pak choi and spring onions, then season to taste.

6. Ladle into bowls and garnish with a pinch chilli flakes before serving.

TOP TIP

Use pre-cooked udon noodles to save time. Simmer for 2 minutes until warm.

Moroccan Chicken Soup

METHOD

1. Heat the olive oil in a large saucepan or casserole dish set over a medium heat until hot.

2. Add the pepper, garlic and a little salt. Sauté for 2 minutes, then stir in the harissa and ras el hanout.

3. Add the chicken thighs and stir again, then add the lentils, chopped tomatoes, chickpeas and stock.

4. Bring the broth to a simmer and cook for 30 minutes, stirring occasionally.

5. Add the noodles after 30 minutes and simmer for a further 10–12 minutes until softened. Remove the chicken thighs and shred the meat before stirring back into the soup.

6. Season the soup with salt and pepper, ladle into bowls and serve.

ES 4

PARATION TIME 10–15 MINUTES

KING TIME 40–45 MINUTES

REDIENTS

sp olive oil
d pepper, deseeded and diced
ves of garlic, minced
and freshly ground black pepper
sp harissa paste
ras el hanout
nless chicken thighs
g / 3 ½ oz / ½ cup green lentils
g / 14 oz / 2 cups canned chopped tomatoes
g / 7 oz / 1 cup canned chickpeas (garbanzo
eans), drained
l / 2 pints 4 fl. oz / 5 cups chicken stock
g / 3 ½ oz / 1 cup vermicelli noodles

TOP TIP

Prepare extra stock, as the beans and pulses will absorb a lot of the liquid.

Prawn and Chilli Soup

MAKES **4**

PREPARATION TIME **15 MINUTES**

COOKING TIME **15–20 MINUTES**

INGREDIENTS

2 tbsp groundnut oil

1 red pepper, deseeded and sliced

1 spring onion (scallion), finely sliced

2 red chillies (chilies), diced

salt and freshly ground black pepper

1.25 l / 2 pints 4 fl. oz / 5 cups fish stock

450 g / 1 lb / 3 cups whole prawns (shrimp),
peeled and deveined

150 g / 5 oz / 2 cups mixed wild mushrooms,
roughly sliced

100 g / 3 ½ oz / 1 cup mangetout

1 lime, juiced

a small handful of coriander (cilantro) leaves,
to garnish

METHOD

1. Heat the oil in a large saucepan set over medium heat until hot.

2. Add the pepper, spring onion, chillies and little salt. Sauté for 2–3 minutes, then co with the stock.

3. Bring to a simmer and cook for 10 minut then add the prawns and mushrooms.

4. Simmer for 4 minutes. Add the mangeto and cook for a further 2 minutes until th prawns are pink and firm to the touch.

5. Add the lime juice to taste and season w salt and pepper.

6. Ladle into bowls and garnish with coriar leaves before serving.

TOP TIP

Thoroughly clean the mushrooms to remove all of the dirt before using.

hai Prawn roth

METHOD

1. Combine the stock, fish sauce, rice wine vinegar, sugar and chilli in a large saucepan set over a moderate heat.

2. Bring to the boil before reducing to a simmer. Add the noodles and cook at a steady simmer for 10–12 minutes until tender.

3. After approximately 5 minutes, add the prawns, peas and mangetout.

4. Once the noodles are ready, add lime juice to taste.

5. Season with salt and pepper before ladling into bowls and serving.

ES 4

PARATION TIME **15 MINUTES**

KING TIME **15–20 MINUTES**

REDIENTS

/ 2 pints 4 fl. oz / 5 cups chicken stock
p fish sauce
p rice wine vinegar
p caster (superfine) sugar
chilli (chili), sliced
/ 5 oz / 1 ½ cups vermicelli noodles
/ 10 ½ oz / 2 cups prawns (shrimp), eeled and deveined
/ 3 ½ oz / 1 cup frozen peas
/ 3 ½ oz / 1 cup mangetout
e, juiced
and freshly ground black pepper

TOP TIP

Whisk the broth at the beginning of the recipe to help dissolve the sugar.

Spicy Beef Soup

SERVES **4**

PREPARATION TIME **10 MINUTES**

COOKING TIME **20 MINUTES**

INGREDIENTS

2 tbsp sesame oil
1 large leek, sliced
1 green chilli (chili), finely chopped
salt and freshly ground black pepper
1.25 l / 2 pints 4 fl. oz / 5 cups beef stock
1 tbsp fish sauce
2 tbsp rice wine vinegar
150 g / 5 oz / 1 ½ cups vermicelli noodles
300 g / 10 ½ oz / 2 cups rump steak, cubed
2 spring onions (scallions), sliced
1 lime, cut into wedges

METHOD

1. Heat the oil in a large saucepan set over medium heat until hot.

2. Add the leek, chilli and a little salt. Sweat 4–5 minutes, then add the stock, fish sauce and rice wine vinegar.

3. Bring to a simmer and add the noodles and beef. Continue to simmer for 10–12 minutes until the noodles are tender.

4. Stir through the spring onions and season to taste.

5. Ladle into bowls and serve with lime wedges on the side.

TOP TIP

For an extra kick, add 1 tbsp of grated ginger to the beef stock.

picy Lamb oup

PARATION TIME **15 MINUTES**

KING TIME **50–55 MINUTES**

REDIENTS

p olive oil

and freshly ground black pepper

g / 1 lb 5 oz / 4 cups boneless lamb shoulder, ubed

on, finely chopped

ves of garlic, minced

p harissa

ras el hanout

g / 5 oz / ⅔ cup green lentils

1 pint 16 fl. oz / 4 cups lamb stock

all bunch of flat-leaf parsley, chopped

METHOD

1. Heat the oil in a large casserole dish set over a moderate heat until hot. Season the lamb and seal in batches until golden all over.

2. Reduce the heat, then add the onion and garlic. Sauté for 3–4 minutes before stirring in the harissa and ras el hanout.

3. Add the lentils, sealed lamb and stock. Stir well and bring to a simmer.

4. Cook at a steady simmer for 35–40 minutes, stirring from time to time, until the lamb is tender. Season to taste before ladling into bowls.

5. Garnish with chopped parsley before serving.

TOP TIP

Add 2 tbsp of the residual fat from the lamb to the onion and garlic.

Curried Lentil Soup

METHOD

1. Heat the oil in a large saucepan set over medium heat until hot.

2. Add the onion, garlic, ginger and a little and sweat for 6–7 minutes. Stir occasion until it starts to brown.

3. Add the ground spices, saving a pinch of curry powder for garnishing. Leave to co for a minute before stirring in the lentils

4. Cover with the stock and bring to the boil for 3 minutes, then reduce to a steady simmer for 20–25 minutes until the lenti are tender.

5. Blend with a stick blender or in a food processor until smooth, then return to th saucepan and gently simmer.

6. Season to taste with salt and pepper, the ladle into bowls and garnish with a pinch curry powder and some coriander leaves

SERVES 4

PREPARATION TIME 10–15 MINUTES

COOKING TIME 35–40 MINUTES

INGREDIENTS

3 tbsp sunflower oil

1 onion, finely chopped

3 cloves of garlic, minced

5 cm (2 in) piece of root ginger,
   peeled and minced

salt and freshly ground black pepper

2 tsp ground cumin

1 tbsp Madras curry powder

½ tsp ground turmeric

1 tsp chilli (chili) powder

250 g / 9 oz / 1 ¼ cups red lentils

1 l / 1 pint 16 fl. oz / 4 cups vegetables stock

a small handful of coriander (cilantro) leaves,
   to garnish

TOP TIP

Remove the residue from the lentil broth, using a large tablespoon or a flat ladle.

quash and azelnut Soup

METHOD

1. Sweat the onion and garlic in the butter in a large pan until golden and soft.

2. Add the squash and cook for five minutes, then add the thyme and stock.

3. Simmer for about 20 minutes or until the squash is tender.

4. Allow to cool a little, then remove the thyme stems and blitz in a food processor or with a stick blender until smooth.

5. Season and stir in the cream. Set aside.

6. Toast the hazelnuts under a hot grill for a few seconds only. Sprinkle on top of the hot soup and serve.

'ES 4

ARATION TIME **10 MINUTES**

ING TIME **40 MINUTES**

REDIENTS

n, peeled and sliced
ic cloves, sliced
butter
je butternut squash, peeled, halved,
seeded and cut into chunks
igs thyme
e chicken or vegetable stock
nd freshly ground black pepper
l / 3 ½ fl oz / ½ cup single cream
l / 3 ½ fl oz / ½ cup hazelnuts (cobnuts),
opped

TOP TIP
Pumpkin works well as an alternative to the squash in this recipe.

Carrot and Cumin Soup

SERVES 4

PREPARATION TIME 15 MINUTES

COOKING TIME 25–30 MINUTES

INGREDIENTS

2 tbsp sunflower oil
1 onion, finely chopped
salt and freshly ground black pepper
750 g / 1 lb 10 oz / 6 cups carrots,
    peeled and sliced
1 large white potato, peeled and diced
1 tbsp ground cumin
1.25 l / 2 pints 4 fl. oz / 5 cups vegetable stock
½ orange, juiced
3 tbsp plain yogurt, to serve
1 tbsp cumin seeds, to garnish

METHOD

1. Heat the oil in a large saucepan set over medium heat until hot.

2. Add the onion and a little salt and sweat for 4–5 minutes, then add the carrot and potato.

3. Cover with a lid and cook for a further 5 minutes, stirring occasionally, until the potato has softened.

4. Stir in the ground cumin and leave to cook for 30 seconds, then cover with the stock.

5. Bring to a simmer and cook for 15 minutes. Blend with a stick blender or in a food processor until smooth.

6. Return to a simmer in the saucepan. Add orange juice to taste and season with salt and pepper.

7. Ladle into bowls and serve with a dollop of yogurt and a garnish of cumin seeds on top.

TOP TIP
The carrot should be soft but not mushy before blending, to retain freshness.

ndian Veggie
oup

ES 4

ARATION TIME **10 MINUTES**

ING TIME **35–40 MINUTES**

REDIENTS

sunflower oil
on, finely chopped
ves of garlic, minced
rots, peeled and chopped
(2 in) piece of root ginger,
eeled and minced
nd freshly ground black pepper
ground cumin
ground coriander (cilantro)
garam masala
/ 5 oz / ⅔ cup red lentils
nl / 1 pint 6 fl. oz / 3 cups vegetable stock
nl / 14 fl. oz / 1 ¾ cups coconut milk

METHOD

1. Heat the oil in a large saucepan set over a medium heat until hot.

2. Add the onion, garlic, carrot, ginger and a little salt. Sauté for 5–6 minutes until they start to brown.

3. Add the ground spices and stir well. Leave to cook for a minute, stirring occasionally.

4. Add the lentils and stir well. Cover with the stock and coconut milk, then bring to the boil and cooking for 5 minutes.

5. Reduce to a simmer for 20–25 minutes until the lentils are tender. Blend with a stick blender or in a food processor until smooth.

6. Return to a simmer in the saucepan and season to taste before serving.

TOP TIP

Wait for the spices and oil mixture to combine before adding to the lentils.

Salads

Salads with Vegetables and Fruit

Goats' Cheese and Fig Salad

SERVES 4

PREPARATION TIME 10 MINUTES

INGREDIENTS

2 fennel bulbs
1 lemon, juiced
salt and freshly ground black pepper
4 ripe figs, thinly sliced
150 g / 5 oz / 1 ½ cups blue goats' cheese
75 ml / 3 fl. oz / ⅓ cup extra virgin olive oil
fennel fronds, reserve for topping

METHOD

1. Remove the fronds from the fennel and roughly chop. Set to one side.

2. Thinly slice the bulbs and toss with the lemon juice, salt and pepper in a large mixing bowl.

3. Add the slices of fig and chopped fronds before tossing again.

4. Crumble in the goats' cheese, then transfer the salad onto bowls.

5. Drizzle with olive oil and serve immediately.

TOP TIP

If the cheese is too soft to crumble, freeze it for 10–15 minutes until firm.

eetroot and
eta Salad

ES 4

ARATION TIME **10 MINUTES**

ING TIME **5 MINUTES**

REDIENTS

buttermilk
mayonnaise
distilled vinegar
nd freshly ground black pepper
flaked (slivered) almonds
all gem lettuce, chopped
/ 14 oz / 2 ⅔ cups cooked beetroot in
negar, drained and diced
/ 3 ½ oz / 1 cup feta
flat-leaf parsley leaves, finely chopped

METHOD

1. Whisk together the buttermilk, mayonnaise
   and vinegar with salt and pepper to make a
   quick dressing.

2. Place the almonds in a dry frying pan set
   over a moderate heat. Once they start to
   toast and brown, tip them onto a plate.

3. Arrange the lettuce and diced beetroot on
   serving plates before crumbling over
   the feta.

4. Drizzle over the dressing and garnish with
   the toasted almonds and parsley
   before serving.

TOP TIP

Make sure you don't
burn the almonds as
this will alter their
nutty taste.

119

Greek Salad

SERVES **4**

PREPARATION TIME **10–15 MINUTES**

INGREDIENTS

1 large green pepper, deseeded and diced
1 large red pepper, deseeded and diced
½ cucumber, peeled, deseeded and diced
½ white onion, finely diced
100 g / 3 ½ oz / ⅔ cup pitted black olives
150 g / 5 oz / 1 ½ cups feta, cubed
3 tbsp extra virgin olive oil
1 lemon, juiced
1 tsp dried oregano
salt and freshly ground black pepper

METHOD

1. Combine the peppers, cucumber, onion, olives and feta in a large mixing bowl.

2. Add the olive oil, lemon juice and a pinch oregano and toss well to combine.

3. Season with salt and pepper, then spoon onto plates.

4. Garnish with the rest of the oregano and serve.

TOP TIP

Use a tablespoon to remove the seeds from the cucumber when preparing it.

mato and
ozzarella
lad

S 4

RATION TIME **4 MINUTES**

DIENTS

lb / 3 cups heirloom tomatoes
freshly ground black pepper
5 oz / 1 ½ cups fresh mozzarella balls,
ned and sliced
alsamic vinegar
oasted sesame seeds, to garnish
bunch of basil, leaves picked

METHOD

1. Remove the top core from the tomatoes using a sharp knife. Cut into generous slices and pile onto serving plates.

2. Season with salt and pepper, then top with slices of mozzarella.

3. Drizzle over the balsamic vinegar, then top with sesame seeds and garnish with basil leaves.

4. Serve immediately for best results.

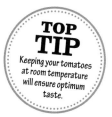

TOP TIP
Keeping your tomatoes at room temperature will ensure optimum taste.

Carrot Salad

METHOD

1. Finely grate the carrots on a mandoli[n]
   julienne setting attached and set to o[ne]

2. Zest the orange into a large mixing bo[wl]
   then halve the orange and juice it into
   the bowl.

3. Add the flaked almonds, walnuts, rais[ins]
   chopped chives, olive oil and seasonir[g]
   Toss briefly.

4. Arrange the salad on plates before to[p]
   with the grated carrot.

5. Grate the apple on the mandolin and s[cat]
   the julienned apple on top of the salad
   before serving.

SERVES 4

PREPARATION TIME 20 MINUTES

INGREDIENTS

6 large carrots, peeled
1 orange
2 tbsp flaked (slivered) almonds
3 tbsp walnuts, chopped
55 g / 2 oz / ⅓ cup raisins or sultanas
a small handful of chive stalks, finely chopped
2 tbsp olive oil
salt and freshly ground black pepper
1 Granny Smith apple, cored

TOP TIP

Place a tea towel
beneath the mandolin
to level it before using.

Waldorf Salad

METHOD

1. Whisk together the yogurt, mayonnaise, lemon juice and seasoning in a mixing bowl until smooth.

2. Add the apple, celery, walnuts and halved grapes, stirring well to coat.

3. Arrange the lettuce leaves in serving bowls and top with the dressed apple, celery, walnuts and grapes. Serve immediately.

VES 4

PARATION TIME 5–10 MINUTES

REDIENTS

p plain yogurt
p mayonnaise
mon, juiced
and freshly ground black pepper
pire or gala apples, cored and diced
cks of celery, sliced
g / 3 ½ oz / 1 cup walnuts
g / 5 oz / 1 cup red seedless grapes, halved
m lettuce, leaves separated

TOP TIP

Peel the celery stalks when preparing them to get rid of the stringy bits.

127

Asparagus Salad

SERVES 4

PREPARATION TIME **10 MINUTES**

COOKING TIME **30–35 MINUTES**

INGREDIENTS

4 small red onions, quartered
3 tbsp olive oil
1 tbsp balsamic vinegar
salt and freshly ground black pepper
a pinch of caster (superfine) sugar
150 g / 5 oz / 1 ½ cups asparagus,
    woody ends removed
2 gem lettuce, quartered
1 orange

METHOD

1. Preheat the oven to 180°C (160°C fan) / [...]
/ gas 4.

2. Arrange the quartered onions in a roast[...]
tray. Drizzle over the olive oil and balsa[...]
vinegar, then sprinkle with the sugar
and seasoning.

3. Toss well and roast for 25–30 minutes u[...]
golden brown at the edges. Remove fro[...]
the oven and leave to cool.

4. Blanch the asparagus spears in a sauce[...]
of salted, boiling water for 2 minutes.
Drain and refresh in iced water.

5. Split most of the spears in half, then slic[...]
the remaining spears across into discs.

6. Arrange the gem lettuce, red onions, an[...]
two kinds of asparagus on serving plate[...]

7. Drizzle over any juices in the roasting tr[...]
and finely grate over some zest from the
orange before serving.

TOP TIP

Add salt to the water before blanching the asparagus.

otato Salad

METHOD

1. Cook the potatoes in a saucepan of salted boiling water for 15–20 minutes until tender to the point of a knife. Drain and leave to cool to one side before slicing.

2. Whisk together the white wine vinegar, mustard, sugar and seasoning in a small mixing bowl.

3. Whisk in the oil in a slow, steady stream until thickened, then stir in the shallot.

4. Toss together the potatoes, dressing, chopped herbs and red onion before serving.

VES 4

PARATION TIME **15 MINUTES**

KING TIME **20–25 MINUTES**

REDIENTS

g / 1 lb 10 oz / 5 cups waxy small
otatoes, peeled
and freshly ground black pepper
p white wine vinegar
wholegrain mustard
ch of caster (superfine) sugar
ml / 4 ½ fl. oz / ½ cup sunflower oil
allot, finely chopped
all bunch of chervil, finely chopped
v chive stalks, finely chopped
d onion, finely sliced

TOP TIP

Stir in 2 tbsp of mayonnaise for a creamy dressing.

Roasted Pepper Salad

SERVES **4**

PREPARATION TIME **10–15 MINUTES**

COOKING TIME **25 MINUTES**

INGREDIENTS

1 large red pepper, deseeded and sliced
1 large yellow pepper, deseeded and sliced
2 tbsp olive oil
salt and freshly ground black pepper
1 romaine lettuce, sliced
2 Braeburn apples, cored and sliced
150 g / 5 oz / 1 cup radishes, roughly chopped
100 g / 3 ½ oz / ⅔ cup cherry tomatoes, halved
55 g / 2 oz / ½ cup cashews, roughly chopped
2 tbsp sunflower seeds
a small handful of micro salad, to garnish
a small bunch of mint, leaves picked

METHOD

1. Preheat the oven to 180°C (160°C fan) / 3
   / gas 4.

2. Toss the peppers with olive oil and
   seasoning, then arrange in a roasting tr

3. Roast for 20 minutes. Remove from the
   and set to one side to cool.

4. Toss together the lettuce, apple, radishe
   cherry tomatoes and cashews in a large
   mixing bowl.

5. Add the peppers and toss again briefly
   before piling onto plates.

6. Garnish with sunflower seeds, micro sa
   and mint leaves before serving.

TOP TIP

Wrap the cashews in a tea towel and bash with a rolling pin for a quick 'chopped' version.

ear and
Walnut Salad

METHOD

1. Toss together the mixed leaf salad with the olive oil and walnuts.

2. Arrange in serving bowls and top with the pear slices, Roquefort and sprigs of chervil.

3. Season with salt and pepper before serving.

VES **4**

PARATION TIME **10 MINUTES**

GREDIENTS

g / 5 oz / 3 cups mixed leaf salad,
washed and dried

sp extra virgin olive oil

/ 3 oz / ¾ cup walnuts

ge conference pears, cored and sliced

g / 3 ½ oz / 1 cup Roquefort, cubed

w sprigs of chervil, to garnish

and freshly ground black pepper

TOP TIP

Using a salad spinner will ensure clean, crisp and dry greens in your salad.

Fennel, Pear and Rocket Salad

SERVES 4

PREPARATION TIME 15 MINUTES

INGREDIENTS

1 fennel (finocchio) bulb, cored and finely sliced
2 ripe pears, cored
2 tbsp lemon juice
250g / 9 oz / 1 cup rocket (arugula) leaves
2 tbsp capers
3 tbsp extra virgin olive oil
salt and freshly ground black pepper

METHOD

1. Place the fennel in a bowl. Thinly slice th
   pears and toss with half the lemon juice
   prevent browning.

2. Scatter the rocket on a platter with
   the capers.

3. Whisk together the oil, remaining lemon
   juice and seasoning and toss with the fe
   and pears.

4. Tip onto the leaves and serve.

TOP TIP

If rocket is too strong use watercress or baby spinach leaves for a milder salad.

tilton and pple Salad

ES 4

ARATION TIME **10 MINUTES**

ING TIME **5 MINUTES**

REDIENTS

sesame seeds
lettuce, leaves separated
/ 7 oz / 2 cups Stilton, sliced
3 oz / 1 cup chestnut mushrooms, sliced
nny Smith apples, cored and sliced
negranate, seeds removed
extra virgin olive oil
ch of paprika
sprigs of chervil, to garnish

METHOD

1. Place the sesame seeds in a dry frying pan and warm over a medium heat until nutty in aroma. Tip into a bowl.

2. Arrange the lettuce leaves on serving plates and top with slices of Stilton, sliced mushrooms, slices of apple and some pomegranate seeds.

3. Drizzle with a little olive oil, then garnish with the toasted sesame seeds, a pinch of paprika and a few sprigs of chervil.

TOP TIP

Cut the pomegranate in half and squeeze the shell to release the seeds.

Courgette and Mint Salad

SERVES 4

PREPARATION TIME 10 MINUTES

COOKING TIME 5 MINUTES

INGREDIENTS

2 tbsp white wine vinegar
¾ tsp Dijon mustard
a pinch of caster (superfine) sugar
salt and freshly ground black pepper
75 ml / 3 fl. oz / ⅓ cup olive oil
2 tbsp pine nuts
2 medium courgettes (zucchinis)
150 g / 5 oz / 1 cup cherry tomatoes, quartered
1 red onion, finely sliced
a large bunch of mint, leaves picked

METHOD

1. Mix together the vinegar, mustard, sug[ar] and seasoning in a small bowl, then wh[isk] the olive oil in a slow, steady stream un[til] you have a thick dressing.

2. Place the pine nuts in a dry frying pan a[nd] toast over a medium heat until aromati[c and] golden. Tip into a bowl.

3. Pass the courgettes over on a mandolin[e with] a julienne setting attached and toss the[se] strands in a little dressing, then pile onto plates.

4. Top with the cherry tomatoes, sliced re[d] onion, pine nuts and mint leaves. Spoon the rest of the dressing.

5. Serve immediately for best results.

TOP TIP

To minimise the strong taste, soak the sliced onion in cold water for 10 minutes first.

reamy
ushroom
alad

ES 4

ARATION TIME **10 MINUTES**

REDIENTS

/ 10 ½ oz / 4 cups button mushrooms
/ 7 oz / 1 cup plain yogurt
mayonnaise
lemon juice
nd freshly ground black pepper
all bunch of chives, finely chopped

METHOD

1. Wash and dry the mushrooms thoroughly,
   then slice.

2. Whisk together the yogurt, mayonnaise,
   lemon juice and seasoning in a small mixing
   bowl until smooth.

3. Arrange the sliced mushrooms in serving
   cups and spoon over the yogurt sauce.

4. Garnish with chopped chives and a little
   more black pepper before serving.

TOP TIP
Instead of chopping the
chives with a knife, snip
them with a pair
of scissors.

Red Cabbage Salad

SERVES 4

PREPARATION TIME 25 MINUTES

INGREDIENTS

2 tbsp olive oil
1 tbsp red wine vinegar
1 tbsp pomegranate molasses
salt and freshly ground black pepper
1 large red cabbage, finely shredded
½ pomegranate, seeds removed
a few chives, finely chopped

METHOD

1. Whisk together the olive oil, red wine vinegar, pomegranate molasses and seasoning in a large mixing bowl.

2. Add the shredded cabbage and toss we[ll]. Cover the bowl with cling film and chill [for] 15 minutes.

3. Divide the chilled salad between bowls garnish with pomegranate seeds and s[o]chives before serving.

TOP TIP

Use a sharp serrated knife to shred the cabbage. A bread knife would be ideal.

Melon and Blue Cheese Salad

SERVES 4

PREPARATION TIME **10 MINUTES**

INGREDIENTS

...sp buttermilk
...sp mayonnaise
...sp warm water
...all cantaloupe melon, deseeded and cut
...nto slices
...d onion, finely sliced
...g / 5 oz / 1 ½ cups cambozola, Brie or
...Roquefort, sliced
...all cucumber, halved and sliced
...all handful of watercress
...nl / 3 fl. oz / ⅓ cup extra virgin olive oil
...ed salt and freshly ground black pepper

METHOD

1. Whisk together the buttermilk and mayonnaise in a small bowl and add enough warm water to thin it out to a pouring consistency.

2. Use a sharp knife to cut the melon flesh away from the skin.

3. Arrange the slices of melon on serving platters along with slices of red onion, cheese, cucumber and some watercress.

4. Drizzle with olive oil and some dressing. Season generously with salt and pepper before serving.

TOP TIP

Use a flexible knife, such as a filleting knife, to remove the skin from the melon.

Grape and Walnut Salad

SERVES 4

PREPARATION TIME 5–10 MINUTES

COOKING TIME 5 MINUTES

INGREDIENTS

2 tbsp pine nuts
55 g / 2 oz / ½ cup walnuts, chopped
55 g / 2 oz / ½ cup orzo pasta, cooked
150 g / 5 oz / 3 cups rocket (arugula)
150 g / 5 oz / 1 cup red seedless grapes, halved
3 tbsp extra virgin olive oil
1 lemon, juiced
salt and freshly ground black pepper
75 g / 3 oz / ¾ cup Parmesan

METHOD

1. Combine the pine nuts and walnuts in a frying pan set over a medium heat. Toast until nutty in aroma before tipping into a bowl.

2. Add the cooked orzo, rocket and grapes and toss with the olive oil, lemon juice and seasoning.

3. Arrange the salad in bowls before shaving over some Parmesan and serving.

TOP TIP

A Y-shaped vegetable peeler is ideal for shaving smaller pieces of cheese.

Salads with Meat and Poultry

Chicken Caesar Salad

SERVES 4

PREPARATION TIME **10 MINUTES**

COOKING TIME **20–25 MINUTES**

INGREDIENTS

2 large skinless chicken breasts, butterflied
150 ml / 5 fl. oz / ⅔ cup sunflower oil
salt and freshly ground black pepper
1 clove of garlic, minced
1 tsp Dijon mustard
1 tbsp white wine vinegar
1 tbsp mayonnaise
4 rashers of bacon
2 slices of sourdough bread
1 large romaine lettuce, chopped
55 g / 2 oz / ½ cup Parmesan, shaved

METHOD

1. Preheat the grill to a moderately high setting. Arrange the butterflied chicken a baking tray and drizzle with a little sunflower oil, then season with salt and pepper.

2. Grill for 12–14 minutes, turning occasion until golden and cooked through.

3. Meanwhile, whisk together the garlic, mustard, vinegar and mayonnaise in a mixing bowl.

4. Add a little seasoning, then whisk in the of the oil in a slow, steady stream until thickened. Cover and set to one side.

5. Remove the chicken from the grill and le to cool.

6. Arrange the bacon on a grilling tray. Gri 4–5 minutes, turning once, until the baco cooked through.

7. Toast the bread, cut into cubes and slice bacon at the same time. Toss the lettuce with the bacon, croutons and some of the dressing before combining with the chic Parmesan and dressing.

TOP TIP

Run your knife down the middle of the chicken breasts before opening out like a book.

hicken Salad

ES 4

ARATION TIME **10 MINUTES**

ING TIME **25–30 MINUTES**

REDIENTS

all skinless chicken breasts

nl / 3 ½ fl. oz / ½ cup olive oil

dried garlic

dried oregano

and freshly ground black pepper

p sherry vinegar

ch of caster (superfine) sugar

/ 5 oz / 3 cups baby spinach, washed

/ 8 oz / 1 ½ cups cherry tomatoes, halved

METHOD

1. Preheat the oven to 180°C (160°C fan) / 350F / gas 4.

2. Arrange the chicken on a baking tray and drizzle with 2 tbsp of olive oil. Season with dried garlic, oregano, salt and pepper.

3. Roast for 20–25 minutes until cooked through.

4. Meanwhile, whisk together the vinegar with the sugar, remaining olive oil and seasoning to make a quick dressing.

5. Remove the chicken from the oven when ready and leave to rest for 5 minutes before slicing.

6. Toss the spinach and cherry tomatoes with the sliced chicken and dressing.

7. Pile onto plates and serve immediately for best results.

TOP TIP

Balsamic or red wine vinegar can also be used instead of sherry vinegar.

Chicken and Grape Salad

SERVES **4**

PREPARATION TIME **10 MINUTES**

COOKING TIME **10 MINUTES**

INGREDIENTS

2 tbsp sunflower oil
2 large skinless chicken breasts, diced
1 tsp paprika
salt and freshly ground black pepper
1 large carrot, peeled
1 round lettuce, chopped
150 g / 5 oz / 1 cup green seedless grapes, halved
75 g / 3 oz / ¾ cup walnuts, chopped

METHOD

1. Heat the oil in a large frying pan set over moderate heat until hot.

2. Season the chicken with paprika, salt and pepper, then sauté in the oil for 7–8 min, tossing and stirring occasionally, until cooked through.

3. Pass the carrot over a mandolin with a julienne setting attached.

4. Arrange the chopped lettuce on plates, top with the carrot, grapes and walnuts.

5. Spoon over the chicken and serve immediately.

TOP TIP

Add a sprinkle of sunflower or pumpkin seeds for extra crunch.

hicken rochette alad

VES **4**

PARATION TIME **10 MINUTES**

KING TIME **20 MINUTES**

REDIENTS

g / 8 oz / 1 ½ cups new potatoes
and freshly ground black pepper
dium chicken breasts, cubed
l / 2 fl. oz / ¼ cup sunflower oil
p honey
g / 5 oz / 3 cups mixed leaf salad
p buttermilk
all handful of chive stalks, chopped
den skewers, soaked in cold water for
0 minutes beforehand

METHOD

1. Cook the potatoes in a large saucepan of salted, boiling water until tender for 15–20 minutes.

2. Meanwhile, preheat the grill to a moderately high temperature. Thread the chicken onto the wooden skewers and brush with oil and honey.

3. Season with salt and pepper, then arrange on a grilling tray and cooking for 8–10 minutes. Turn occasionally, until golden and cooked through.

4. Drain the potatoes when ready and leave to cool before slicing.

5. Arrange the salad on plates and top with slices of potato, chicken brochettes, a drizzle of buttermilk and some chives.

TOP TIP

Warming the honey before brushing onto the chicken will help it spread.

Ham and Rocket Salad

SERVES **4**

PREPARATION TIME **10 MINUTES**

INGREDIENTS

110 ml / 4 fl. oz / ½ cup extra virgin olive oil
2 tbsp white wine vinegar
1 tsp Dijon mustard
½ tsp honey
salt and freshly ground black pepper
1 shallot, finely chopped
150 g / 5 oz / 3 cups rocket (arugula)
200 g / 7 oz / 1 ⅓ cups prosciutto slices
250 g / 9 oz / 1 ⅔ cups mixed cherry tomatoes,
    halved
300 g / 10 ½ oz / 2 cups baby mozzarella balls,
    drained

METHOD

1. Shake together the olive oil, vinegar,
   mustard, honey and seasoning in an em
   jar or salad shaker.

2. Add the shallot and shake again.

3. Arrange the rocket leaves, prosciutto, ch
   tomatoes and mozzarella on serving pla

4. Spoon over the dressing and season wit
   salt and pepper before serving.

TOP TIP
Shake the dressing again just before serving if it starts to separate.

Iam and Cheese Salad

METHOD

1. Whisk together the olive oil, balsamic vinegar, sugar and salt and pepper in a large mixing bowl.

2. Add the mixed leaf salad and toss well to coat.

3. Add the chicken slices and toss again before dividing between serving plates.

4. Top with the prosciutto, Emmental and sun-dried tomatoes before serving.

RVES 4

PARATION TIME 10 MINUTES

GREDIENTS

- nl / 2 fl. oz / ¼ cup olive oil
- sp balsamic vinegar
- nch of caster (superfine) sugar
- and freshly ground black pepper
- g / 5 oz / 3 cups mixed leaf salad
- g / 7 oz / 1 ⅓ cups cooked chicken breast, sliced
- g / 5 oz / 1 cup prosciutto slices
- g / 7 oz / 2 cups Emmental, cut into blocks
- / 3 oz / ½ cup sun-dried tomatoes in oil, drained and roughly chopped

TOP TIP

Remove the hard rind from the Emmental before cutting into blocks.

Italian Antipasti Platter

SERVES 4

PREPARATION TIME 15 MINUTES

COOKING TIME 10–15 MINUTES

INGREDIENTS

110 ml / 4 fl. oz / ½ cup extra virgin olive oil

a small bunch of flat-leaf parsley, finely chopped

1 clove of garlic, minced

salt and freshly ground black pepper

1 aubergine (eggplant), sliced into strips

1 orange pepper, roughly sliced

1 red pepper, deseeded and roughly sliced

55 ml / 2 fl. oz / ¼ cup olive oil

200 g / 7 oz / 1 cup mascarpone

400 g / 14 oz / 2 cups cherry peppers in oil, drained

400 g / 14 oz / 2 cups canned artichoke hearts, drained

100 g / 3 ½ oz / ⅔ cup preserved anchovy fillets, drained

75 g / 3 oz / ½ cup pitted black olives

a few sprigs of chervil, to garnish

METHOD

1. Preheat a griddle pan over a moderate heat until hot. Whisk together the extra virgin olive oil, parsley, garlic and seasoning in a small mixing bowl and set to one side.

2. Brush the aubergine and peppers with the olive oil. Season with salt and pepper before grilling until lightly charred all over.

3. Remove from the griddle pan and set to one side.

4. Spoon the mascarpone into the cherry peppers and set to one side.

5. Arrange the griddled peppers, aubergine, stuffed peppers, artichoke hearts, anchovy fillets and black olives on a platter.

6. Pour over the prepared parsley oil and garnish with chervil before serving.

TOP TIP

Trim any bones from the anchovy fillets before serving.

Bacon and Egg Salad

SERVES 4

PREPARATION TIME 5–10 MINUTES

COOKING TIME 10 MINUTES

INGREDIENTS

rashers of back bacon
large eggs
bsp buttermilk
bsp mayonnaise
tbsp lemon juice
clove of garlic, minced
lt and freshly ground black pepper
0 g / 3 ½ oz / 2 cups mixed leaf salad

METHOD

1. Preheat the grill to hot and arrange the bacon on a grilling tray.

2. Bring a large saucepan of water to the boil. Carefully lower the eggs into the water and cook for 9 minutes.

3. Meanwhile, grill the bacon for 4–5 minutes, turning once, until golden and crisp. Remove and drain on kitchen paper.

4. Drain the eggs once cooked and refresh immediately in iced water.

5. Whisk together the buttermilk, mayonnaise, lemon juice, garlic and seasoning in a small bowl.

6. Arrange the salad on plates and top with the bacon. Peel the eggs and cut in half before arranging on the plates.

7. Spoon over the dressing and season with black pepper before serving.

TOP TIP

Refresh the eggs immediately after draining in a bowl of iced water.

Duck and Stilton Salad

SERVES 4

PREPARATION TIME 10–15 MINUTES

COOKING TIME 25 MINUTES

INGREDIENTS

salt and freshly ground black pepper
2 large duck breasts, trimmed and scored
100 g / 3 ½ oz / 2 cups lamb's lettuce
100 g / 3 ½ oz / 1 cup Stilton, sliced
2 spring onions (scallions), finely sliced
150 g / 5 oz / 1 cup yellow cherry tomatoes,
    halved
2 radishes, thinly sliced

METHOD

1. Preheat the oven to 180°C (160°C fan) / 350F / gas 4.

2. Season the duck breasts and lay skin-side down in a dry frying pan. Place the frying pan over a medium heat.

3. Once most of the fat has rendered from the breasts, flip them over and cook for 1 minute before transferring to the oven to finish cooking for 6–8 minutes.

4. Remove from the oven and transfer to a warm plate to rest for 10 minutes.

5. Arrange the lettuce, Stilton, spring onion, cherry tomatoes and radish on serving plate

6. Slice the duck breasts and add to the salad before serving.

TOP TIP

Use a sharp knife to make a crosshatch pattern in the fat of the duck breasts.

loughman's alad

VES 4

PARATION TIME **40 MINUTES**

KING TIME **1 HOUR 15-30 MINUTES**

REDIENTS

g / 7 oz / 1 cup lard

ml / 9 fl. oz / 1 cup hot water

g / 1 lb 10 oz / 5 cups plain (all-purpose) flour,
us extra for dusting

and freshly ground black pepper

g / 1 lb 5 oz / 4 cups pork mince

dium egg, lightly beaten

g / 3 ½ oz / ⅔ cup mimolette

g / 7 oz / 1 ⅓ cups cashel blue or other
lue cheese

e vine tomatoes

all head of round lettuce, leaves separated

olemeal loaf

ed onions in vinegar, to serve

METHOD

1. Preheat the oven to 180°C (160°C fan) / 350F / gas 4. Place the lard and water in a saucepan set over a moderate heat and bring to the boil.

2. Combine the flour and a pinch of salt in a food processor. Add the lard mixture, mixing at the same time, until you have a smooth dough. Turn out two-thirds onto a floured surface. Cover the remaining third with a tea towel.

3. Roll the large piece out to 1 cm (½ in) thickness and cut out 2 rounds approximately 15 cm (6 in). Lift the rounds into 12 cm (5 in) pork pie moulds. The pastry should overhang slightly.

4. Fill the cases with the pork mince and seasoning. Roll out the rest of the pastry to 1 cm (½ in) thickness and cut out two pastry lids. Wet the rims with some egg and seal well before brushing the tops with more egg. Bake for 1 hour 15–30 minutes until the pork pies are golden and cooked.

5. Remove from the oven and leave to cool before serving with the remaining ingredients on platters.

TOP TIP

The pork pies can be served warm from the oven or left to cool.

Veal Salad

SERVES 4

PREPARATION TIME 20 MINUTES

COOKING TIME 15 MINUTES

INGREDIENTS

2 large white potatoes, peeled and cubed
salt and freshly ground black pepper
2 tbsp sunflower oil
2 x 250 g / 9 oz rose veal steaks, trimmed
1 tbsp unsalted butter
150 g / 5 oz / 1 ½ cups frozen peas, thawed
75 ml / 3 fl. oz / ⅓ cup extra virgin olive oil
2 tbsp balsamic vinegar
1 tsp honey
2 gem lettuce, chopped
a small handful of flat-parsley leaves, to garnish

METHOD

1. Preheat the oven to 190°C (170°C fan) / 3 / gas 5.

2. Cook the potato in a large saucepan of salted, boiling water for 4–5 minutes unt tender to the point of a knife. Drain and le to cool.

3. Heat the oil in a large frying pan set over moderate heat until hot.

4. Season the veal steaks and seal for 1 mir on both sides. Top with the butter and transfer to the oven for 4 minutes. Trans to a warm plate and rest for 10 minutes.

5. Blanch the peas in a large saucepan of salted, boiling water for 2 minutes. Drain and leave to cool.

6. Whisk together the olive oil, balsamic vinegar, honey and seasoning to make a quick dressing.

7. Combine the chopped lettuce, potato and peas in a large mixing bowl. Add the dressing and toss well.

8. Arrange on plates and slice the veal into strips before adding to the salad. Garnish with parsley leaves before servin

TOP TIP

Resting the veal steaks for 10 minutes will help them retain the juices.

horizo and each Salad

VES 4

PARATION TIME 10 MINUTES

KING TIME 10 MINUTES

REDIENTS

g / 5 oz / 1 cup chorizo

aches, pitted and quartered

and freshly ground black pepper

sp olive oil

g / 10 ½ oz / 3 cups green (string) beans

p white wine vinegar

Dijon mustard

ch of caster (superfine) sugar

ml / 4 fl. oz / ½ cup sunflower oil

ing onions (scallions), sliced

METHOD

1. Peel the chorizo and cut into small batons. Set to one side.

2. Preheat a griddle pan over a moderate heat until hot. Brush the peaches with olive oil and season, then griddle until lightly charred.

3. Meanwhile, bring a large saucepan of salted water to the boil. Cook the beans for 3 minutes before draining and setting to one side.

4. Whisk together the vinegar, mustard, sugar and seasoning in a small mixing bowl. Whisk in the sunflower oil in a slow, steady stream until you have a thick dressing.

5. Arrange the beans on serving plates and spoon over some of the dressing.

6. Top with the peaches, chorizo and a sprinkling of spring onions. Serve with the rest of the dressing on the side.

TOP TIP

Run the tip of a sharp knife down the length of the chorizo to remove the skin.

Steak Salad

SERVES **4**

PREPARATION TIME **10 MINUTES**

COOKING TIME **15 MINUTES**

INGREDIENTS

2 tbsp sunflower oil
salt and freshly ground black pepper
2 x 250 g / 9 oz rump or sirloin steaks, trimmed
110 ml / 4 fl. oz / ½ cup extra virgin olive oil
2 tbsp balsamic vinegar
½ tsp dried oregano
1 clove of garlic, minced
150 g / 5 oz / 3 cups mixed leaf salad
1 green pepper, deseeded and sliced
1 small red onion, finely sliced
2 large plum tomatoes, chopped

METHOD

1. Heat the sunflower oil in a large frying pan set over a moderate heat until hot.

2. Season the steak and fry for 3–4 minutes both sides for medium-rare. Remove from the pan and leave to rest in a warm place at least 5 minutes.

3. Whisk together the olive oil, balsamic vinegar, oregano, garlic and seasoning to make a quick dressing.

4. Slice the steak and arrange on plates. Toss together the salad, pepper, red onion and tomato in a mixing bowl before serving alongside the steak.

5. Serve with pots of the dressing on the side.

TOP TIP
Cut around any gristle
or membrane in the
rump steak as
you slice.

Turkey Tikka Salad

SERVES 4

PREPARATION TIME **10 MINUTES**

COOKING TIME **10 MINUTES**

INGREDIENTS

2 tbsp sunflower oil

Salt and freshly ground black pepper

400 g / 14 oz / 2 ²/₃ cups turkey steaks in
tikka marinade

2 tbsp plain yogurt

2 tbsp mayonnaise

1 lemon, juiced

200 g / 7 oz / 4 cups mixed leaf salad

METHOD

1. Heat the oil in a large frying pan set over
a moderate heat until hot.

2. Season the turkey steaks and fry for
5–6 minutes, turning once, until golden
all over and firm to the touch.

3. Remove from the pan and leave to rest for a
few minutes before dicing.

4. Whisk together the yogurt, mayonnaise,
lemon juice and seasoning.

5. Arrange the salad on plates and top with
the turkey and a drizzle of the dressing
before serving.

TOP TIP

Turn the steaks after
4 minutes when you
start to see their
tops cooking.

Turkey and Mango Salad

SERVES 4

PREPARATION TIME 15 MINUTES

COOKING TIME 10 MINUTES

INGREDIENTS

3 tbsp plain yogurt
1 tbsp mayonnaise
½ lemon, juiced
1 tsp Dijon mustard
salt and freshly ground black pepper
2 tbsp sunflower oil
2 large turkey breasts steaks, sliced
4 sticks of celery, chopped
1 large ripe mango, pitted and sliced
2 tbsp cashews, roughly chopped
a small bunch of flat-leaf parsley,
    roughly chopped

METHOD

1. Whisk together the yogurt, mayonnaise, lemon juice, mustard and seasoning to make a quick dressing.

2. Heat the oil in a large frying pan set over a moderate heat until hot. Season the turkey and fry for 5–6 minutes, until cooked through.

3. Remove from the pan and leave to cool slightly before tossing with the celery, mango, cashews and parsley.

4. Spoon onto plates and spoon over a little of the dressing before serving.

TOP TIP

When preparing the mango, use a flexible filleting knife to work around the stone.

Salads with Fish and Seafood

Prawn and Avocado Salad

SERVES 4

PREPARATION TIME 10–15 MINUTES

INGREDIENTS

2 medium ripe avocados, pitted
2 oranges, peeled and segmented
salt and freshly ground black pepper
300 g / 10 ½ oz / 2 cups cooked,
    peeled prawns (shrimp)
2 tbsp olive oil
½ lemon, juiced
a few rocket (arugula) leaves, to garnish

METHOD

1. Remove the skin from the avocados and thinly slice the flesh.

2. Place the avocado in a mixing bowl with the oranges and season with salt and pepper.

3. Arrange in serving bowls. Toss the prawns with the olive oil, lemon juice and seasoning.

4. Spoon on top of the avocado and orange before garnishing with rocket and serving.

TOP TIP
Use a flexible knife, such as a filleting knife, for segmenting the oranges.

Smoked Salmon Salad

SERVES 4

PREPARATION TIME 15 MINUTES

INGREDIENTS

cucumber, halved and deseeded

0 g / 7 oz / 2 cups feta

0 g / 10 ½ oz / 2 cups smoked salmon, sliced

emon, juiced

lt and freshly ground black pepper

bsp baby capers, drained

ew sprigs of chervil, roughly chopped

METHOD

1. Fit a mandolin with a julienne setting. Pass the cucumber over the mandolin and collect the strands.

2. Cut the feta into blocks and place on serving plates.

3. Dress the smoked salmon with the lemon juice and some pepper before folding and draping over the feta.

4. Top with the strands of cucumber before garnishing with capers, chervil, salt and pepper.

TOP TIP

Both the feta and salmon are very salty. Adjust the seasoning accordingly.

Chilli Crab Salad

METHOD

1. Whisk together the olive oil, vinegar, chilli, chopped herbs and seasoning to make a quick dressing.

2. Add the dressing to the avocado, greens, grapefruit, olives and crabmeat in a large mixing bowl.

3. Toss well before spooning into serving bowls.

4. Garnish with a sprinkling of chopped almonds before serving.

SERVES 4

PREPARATION TIME 10 MINUTES

INGREDIENTS

110 ml / 4 fl. oz / ½ cup olive oil

2 tbsp white wine vinegar

1 red chilli (chili), finely chopped

a small bunch of flat-leaf parsley, finely chopped

a few chive stalks, chopped

salt and freshly ground black pepper

1 large avocado, pitted, peeled and diced

200 g / 7 oz / 4 cups lamb's lettuce or winter purslane (if available)

1 red grapefruit, peeled, segmented and chopped

75 g / 3 oz / ½ cup manzanilla olives in brine, drained

250 g / 9 oz / 1 ⅔ cups cooked white crabmeat

2 tbsp almonds, chopped

TOP TIP

Deseed the chilli for less heat in the dressing.

Crab and Bacon Salad

SERVES 4

PREPARATION TIME 10–15 MINUTES

COOKING TIME 5 MINUTES

INGREDIENTS

- ml / 4 fl. oz / ½ cup olive oil
- lemon, juiced
- ed chilli (chili), finely chopped
- large handful of chervil, finely chopped
- t and freshly ground black pepper
- ashers of streaky bacon
- g / 9 oz / 1 ⅔ cups cooked white crabmeat
- nk grapefruit, peeled,
  segmented and chopped
- ocado, pitted, peeled and diced
- g / 3 ½ oz / 2 cups mixed leaf salad
- mall cucumber, cut into thin strips

METHOD

1. Whisk together the olive oil, half the lemon juice, the chilli, some of the chervil and seasoning in a mixing bowl.

2. Preheat the grill to hot and grill the bacon for 4–5 minutes, turning once, until golden. Remove and drain on kitchen paper.

3. Place the bacon in a food processor and pulse briefly to chop. Add the crabmeat, remaining chervil, lemon juice and some pepper before pulsing again until just combined.

4. Dress the grapefruit, avocado and mixed leaf salad with the rest of the dressing, then transfer to plates.

5. Top with the crab mixture and cucumber strips before serving.

TOP TIP

For best results, take care to not over mix the crab meat in the food processor.

Herring and Apple Salad

SERVES **4**

PREPARATION TIME **10 MINUTES**

COOKING TIME **10 MINUTES**

INGREDIENTS

2 Granny Smith apples, cored and sliced
2 slices of sourdough bread, cubed
3 tbsp olive oil
salt and freshly ground black pepper
300 g / 10 ½ oz / 2 cups canned herring
    fillets, drained
a small bunch of chervil, roughly chopped
a small bunch of dill, roughly chopped
a large handful of rocket (arugula)
2 tbsp extra virgin olive oil

METHOD

1. Preheat the grill to a moderately high temperature. Toss the apple slices and cubed bread with the olive oil and seasonin

2. Spread out on a grilling tray and toast unde the grill until lightly browned all over.

3. Remove from the grill and leave to cool slightly before arranging on plates with the herring fillets.

4. Top with the chervil, dill and rocket. Garnish with a drizzle of extra virgin olive and some seasoning before serving.

TOP TIP
Check the herring fillets for bones or cartilage before serving.

Smoked Trout Salad

METHOD

1. Cook the eggs in a saucepan of boiling water for 10 minutes. Drain and refresh in cold water.

2. Once cool enough to handle, peel and cut into wedges.

3. Spoon the rice onto plates and top with cherry tomatoes and flaked trout. Garnish with parsley and egg before serving.

RVES 4

EPARATION TIME **10 MINUTES**

OKING TIME **15 MINUTES**

GREDIENTS

edium eggs

g / 10 ½ oz / 2 cups cooked pilau rice, cold

g / 8 oz / 1 ½ cups cherry tomatoes, halved

g / 9 oz / 1 ²/₃ cups cooked smoked trout

fillets, flaked

w sprigs of flat-leaf parsley, roughly chopped

TOP TIP

Add 1 tbsp of capers for a naturally salty, fresh taste.

Warm Mackerel Salad

SERVES **4**

PREPARATION TIME **10 MINUTES**

COOKING TIME **10 MINUTES**

INGREDIENTS

4 mackerel fillets
2 tbsp olive oil
salt and freshly ground black pepper
400 g / 14 oz / 2 ⅔ cups cooked orzo pasta
1 small head of radicchio, shredded
2 tbsp extra virgin olive oil
1 lemon, juiced
a small handful of cress, chopped
55 g / 2 oz / ¼ cup sunflower seeds

METHOD

1. Preheat the grill to hot. Arrange the mackerel fillets on a grilling tray and drizzle with olive oil before seasoning.

2. Grill for 4–5 minutes until the flesh is firm to the touch. Remove and leave to cool.

3. Once cool enough to handle, remove the flesh from any bone or skin.

4. Toss the orzo with the radicchio, extra virgin olive oil, lemon juice, cress and 2 tbsp of sunflower seeds. Season to taste and spoon onto plates.

5. Top with the mackerel before serving with more sunflower seeds on the side.

TOP TIP

To serve the salad warm, reheat the orzo before adding the remaining ingredients.

Niçoise Salad

SERVES 4

PREPARATION TIME 10 MINUTES

COOKING TIME 20–25 MINUTES

INGREDIENTS

- 00 g / 10 ½ oz / 2 cups new potatoes
- alt and freshly ground black pepper
- large eggs
- 00 g / 10 ½ oz / 2 cups tuna fillet
- 0 ml / 4 fl oz / ½ cup olive oil
- tbsp white wine vinegar
- sp Dijon mustard
- slices of white bread
- 5 g / 8 oz / 2 cups green (string) beans
- vine tomatoes, cored and quartered
- g / 3 oz / ½ cup pitted black olives, sliced
- bsp capers
- 0 g / 3 ½ oz / ⅔ cup anchovy fillets, drained

METHOD

1. Preheat the grill to a moderately hot temperature. Cook the potatoes in a large saucepan of salted, boiling water until tender to the point of a knife for 15–20 minutes, then drain.

2. Lower the eggs into a saucepan of boiling water. Cook for 12 minutes. Drain and refresh in iced water.

3. Brush the tuna with 2 tbsp of olive oil, then season and grill for 4 minutes. Turn after 2 minutes. Remove from the grill and leave to rest for a few minutes.

4. Whisk together the white wine vinegar, mustard and seasoning in a small bowl. Add the remaining olive oil until you have a thick dressing.

5. Toast the bread in a toaster. Cut into cubes and peel and quarter the eggs.

6. Blanch the green beans in a saucepan of salted water for 3 minutes. Drain and arrange on serving plates along with the tomato, croutons, black olives, capers and anchovy fillets.

7. Slice the potatoes and tuna before adding to the salad; spoon over the dressing before serving.

TOP TIP

Prepare a couple of bowls of iced water to refresh the eggs and green beans.

Salads with Beans, Grains and Pasta

Lemon and Coriander Couscous

SERVES 4

PREPARATION TIME **10 MINUTES**

COOKING TIME **15–20 MINUTES**

INGREDIENTS

175 g / 6 oz / 1 cup couscous
salt and freshly ground black pepper
110 g / 4 oz / 1 cup asparagus spears,
    woody ends removed
150 g / 5 oz / 1 ½ cups broad (fava) beans, shelled
1 lemon, juiced
75 g / 3 oz / ½ cup sun-dried tomatoes in oil,
    drained and chopped
a small bunch of coriander (cilantro), roughly
    chopped
a small handful of mint leaves
a pinch of crushed red peppercorns
½ lime, sliced

METHOD

1. Place the couscous in a heatproof mixing bowl, then cover with boiling water.

2. Cover the bowl with cling film and set to one side for 10–15 minutes, until the water has been completely absorbed.

3. Meanwhile, bring a large saucepan of salted water to boiling point. Blanch the asparagus for 2 minutes, then remove from the water with tongs.

4. Add the broad beans to the water and cook for 2 minutes before draining.

5. Fluff the couscous with a fork and stir through the lemon juice and seasoning. Spoon into bowls.

6. Split the asparagus spears and add them to the salad with the broad beans, sun-dried tomatoes and herbs. Garnish with crushed red peppercorns and slices of lime before serving.

TOP TIP

If the couscous is too wet, microwave in 30-second intervals until dry.

Italian Bean Salad

SERVES 4

PREPARATION TIME 25 MINUTES

COOKING TIME 8 MINUTES

INGREDIENTS

1 red pepper, deseeded and sliced
1 green pepper, deseeded and sliced
1 yellow pepper, deseeded and sliced
1 orange pepper, deseeded and sliced
150 ml / 5 fl. oz / ⅔ cup olive oil
salt and freshly ground black pepper
2 cloves of garlic, minced
350 g / 12 oz / 3 cups broad (fava) beans, shelled
225 g / 8 oz / 2 cups peas
75 g / 2 oz / ½ cup hard Italian cheese
   (e.g. Parmesan, Asiago)

METHOD

1. Preheat the oven to 180°C (160°C fan) / 350F / gas 4.

2. Toss the peppers with a third of the olive oil. Season with salt and pepper, then tip into a roasting tray and roast for 25 minutes until soft.

3. Remove from the oven and transfer the orange pepper to a food processor.

4. Add the garlic and blend as you add the rest of the olive oil.

5. Bring a large saucepan of salted water to the boil and cook the broad beans and peas for 3 minutes. Drain and leave to cool.

6. Toss the broad beans and peas with the roasted peppers and seasoning. Divide between bowls.

7. Top with the orange pepper pesto and shavings of cheese before serving.

TOP TIP

Add the oil to the food processor as you prepare the pesto. It should make a purée.

205

Warm Thai Noodle Salad

SERVES **4**

PREPARATION TIME **10–15 MINUTES**

COOKING TIME **20 MINUTES**

INGREDIENTS

2 small duck breasts, scored

2 tbsp groundnut oil

2 tbsp fish sauce

3 tbsp rice wine vinegar

2 tbsp water

1 lime, juiced

1 tbsp caster (superfine) sugar

350 g / 3 oz / 3 cups egg noodles, cooked

2 spring onions (scallions), sliced

110 g / 4 oz / ½ cup canned water chestnuts, drained

55 g / 2 oz / 1 cup crispy seaweed, soaked in hot water and drained

salt and freshly ground black pepper

a few sprigs of coriander (cilantro), to garnish

METHOD

1. Place the duck breasts skin-side down in a dry frying pan. Set over a medium heat and cook until most of the fat has rendered away.

2. Drain away any excess fat and flip the duck breasts, continuing to cook them for 6–8 minutes until firm yet slightly springy to the touch. Remove from the pan and leave to rest.

3. Whisk together the groundnut oil, fish sauce, vinegar, water, lime juice and sugar in a large saucepan. Bring to a simmer over a low heat.

4. Add the noodles, spring onions, water chestnuts and seaweed. Toss to coat well.

5. Slice the duck breasts and add to the noodles, tossing again before seasoning to taste.

6. Lift into bowls and garnish with coriander before serving.

TOP TIP

Check the temperature of the duck with a meat thermometer; it should read 74°C / 165F.

Bulgur and Beetroot Salad

SERVES 4

PREPARATION TIME 5 MINUTES

COOKING TIME 25–30 MINUTES

INGREDIENTS

150 g / 5 oz / ⅔ cup bulgur wheat, rinsed
250 ml / 9 fl. oz / 1 cup vegetable stock
150 g / 5 oz / ⅔ cup green lentils
cooked beetroot in vinegar, drained and sliced
100 g / 3 ½ oz / 2 cups Swiss chard or
    beetroot leaves
100 g / 3 ½ oz / 1 cup feta, crumbled
salt and freshly ground black pepper

METHOD

1. Combine the bulgur wheat and stock in a saucepan. Bring to a simmer and cook over a reduced heat, stirring frequently, until the bulgur has absorbed the liquid. Set to one side.

2. Place the lentils in a saucepan and cover by 5 cm (2 in) of hot water. Bring to boiling point, then simmer steadily for 15–20 minutes until tender.

3. Drain the lentils and leave to cool.

4. Once the lentils and bulgur wheat are cool, assemble the salad by placing the greens on serving plates.

5. Top with bulgur wheat, lentils and sliced beetroot.

6. Season with salt and pepper before serving.

TOP TIP
Add more water to the lentils as they cook, to prevent them drying out.

Moroccan Chickpea Salad

SERVES 4

PREPARATION TIME 5–10 MINUTES

COOKING TIME 20–25 MINUTES

INGREDIENTS

600 g / 1 lb 5 oz / 3 cups canned chickpeas
    (garbanzo beans), drained
1 large red onion, finely sliced
1 preserved lemon, drained and chopped
75 ml / 3 fl. oz / ⅓ cup olive oil
1 lemon, juiced
a small bunch of flat-leaf parsley, chopped
salt and freshly ground black pepper

METHOD

1. Place the chickpeas in a large saucepan and cover with at least 5 cm (2 in) of cold water. Bring to boiling point over a moderate heat before reducing to a steady simmer.

2. Cook for 15–20 minutes until tender. Drain and leave to cool slightly before tossing with the remaining ingredients.

3. Season accordingly and spoon into bowls before serving.

TOP TIP

Discard any chickpea shells that rise to the surface as they cook.

Exotic Rice Salad

SERVES 4

PREPARATION TIME 15 MINUTES

COOKING TIME 20–25 MINUTES

INGREDIENTS

150 g / 5 oz / 1 cup long grain rice, rinsed

110 ml / 4 fl. oz / ½ cup extra virgin olive oil

2 tbsp balsamic vinegar

½ small red onion, finely chopped

pinch of caster (superfine) sugar

salt and freshly ground black pepper

large handful of Swiss chard or beetroot leaves

pomegranate

150 g / 5 oz / 1 cup yellow cherry tomatoes, halved

avocado, pitted, peeled and thinly sliced

small cucumber, thinly sliced

METHOD

1. Cook the rice according to packet instructions. Drain and leave to cool before chilling until cold.

2. Whisk together the olive oil, balsamic vinegar, red onion, sugar and seasoning. Set to one side.

3. Slice a few of the chard leaves and set to one side.

4. Halve the pomegranate and firmly tap the skin side of each half with a wooden spoon to release the seeds.

5. Fluff the rice with a fork and toss with the chard, pomegranate seeds, cherry tomatoes, avocado and cucumber in a large salad bowl.

6. Spoon into serving bowls and dress with the dressing and a little more black pepper before serving.

TOP TIP

Look out for rainbow chard for a colourful addition to this salad.

Tomato and Feta Pasta Salad

SERVES 4

PREPARATION TIME 5–10 MINUTES

COOKING TIME 15 MINUTES

INGREDIENTS

salt and freshly ground black pepper
350 g / 12 oz / 3 cups fusilli pasta
150 g / 5 oz / 1 cup cherry tomatoes, halved
3 tbsp basil pesto
100 g / 3 ½ oz / ⅔ cup pitted black olives,
    chopped
55 g / 2 oz / ½ cup feta

METHOD

1. Bring a large saucepan of salted water to the boil. Cook the pasta for 8–10 minutes until 'al dente' before draining.

2. Leave to cool for 5 minutes before tossing with the cherry tomatoes, pesto and olives in a large mixing bowl. Season to taste.

3. Spoon into bowls and shave over some feta before serving.

TOP TIP

Use approximately 1 ½ tsp of salt per litre of water for cooking pasta.

Tuna and Bean Salad

SERVES 4

PREPARATION TIME **10 MINUTES**

COOKING TIME **30–35 MINUTES**

INGREDIENTS

110 g / 4 oz / 1 cup green (string) beans
150 g / 5 oz / 1 ½ cups farfalle pasta
4 large eggs
300 g / 10 ½ oz / 2 cups tuna steak
1 tbsp olive oil
salt and freshly ground black pepper
100 g / 3 ½ oz / ⅔ cup cherry tomatoes, halved
75 g / 3 oz / ½ cup pitted black olives, sliced
1 shallot, thinly sliced
1 tbsp sesame seeds

METHOD

1. Bring a large saucepan of salted water to the boil. Blanch the green beans for 3 minutes, then remove to a bowl of cold water with a pair of tongs.

2. Return the water to the boil and cook the pasta for 8–10 minutes until al dente, then drain and leave to cool to one side.

3. Cook the eggs in a saucepan of boiling water for 12 minutes. Drain and refresh in cold water.

4. Preheat the grill to hot. Brush the tuna steak with olive oil and season with salt and pepper.

5. Grill for 4 minutes, turning once halfway through. Remove from the grill and leave to rest in a warm place for a few minutes.

6. Peel the eggs and cut into wedges, then assemble them on platters with the beans, pasta, cherry tomatoes, olives and shallot.

7. Slice the tuna and place on top of the salad. Garnish with sesame seeds before serving.

TOP TIP

Add more water and salt to the saucepan after the beans have cooked for the pasta.

Soba Noodle Salad

METHOD

1. Whisk together the rice wine vinegar, soy sauce and rice wine in a large mixing bowl.

2. Steam the edamame in a covered steaming basket set over a saucepan of simmering water. Cook for 8–10 minutes until tender.

3. Shell the edamame beans into the dressing in the mixing bowl. Add the remaining ingredients. Toss well.

4. Serve in bowls.

SERVES 4

PREPARATION TIME 10–15 MINUTES

COOKING TIME 20–25 MINUTES

INGREDIENTS

2 tbsp groundnut oil
110 g / 4 oz / 1 cup edamame beans
3 tbsp rice wine vinegar
2 tbsp dark soy sauce
1 tbsp rice wine
a small bunch of coriander (cilantro),
    finely chopped
3 large carrots, peeled and shredded
1 red onion, thinly sliced
1 yellow pepper, finely diced
1 red pepper, finely diced
350 g / 10 ½ oz / 3 cups cooked soba noodles
salt and freshly ground black pepper

TOP TIP
Make sure the steaming basket does not touch the simmering water.